MILLER ANALOGIES TEST

1400

ANALOGY QUESTIONS

PROGRAMMED

by

DAVID R. TURNER, M.S. in Ed.

arco   219 Park Avenue South
New York, N.Y. 10003

Third Edition (B-1497)
Thirteenth Printing, 1981

Copyright © 1973
by Arco Publishing, Inc.

Published by Arco Publishing, Inc.
219 Park Avenue South, New York, N. Y. 10003

Library of Congress Catalog Card Number 72-000050
ISBN 0-668-01115-7 (Library Edition)
ISBN 0-668-01114-9 (Paper Edition)

Printed in the United States of America

CONTENTS

HOW TO USE THIS INDEX
Slightly bend the right-hand edge
of the book. This will expose
the corresponding Parts
which match the index, below.

PART

1

2

3

4

...continued on next page

CONTENTS continued

PART

1

2

3

4

PART THREE

THREE SAMPLE MILLER ANALOGIES TESTS

PART FOUR

NONVERBAL ANALOGY TESTS
REASONING ABILITY PRACTICE
FINAL ADVICE

INTRODUCTION

How this Book is Divided

Part One, "Essential Information About Analogies," first tells you how to use this new-type book that works like a teaching machine. Also in Part One you will find common forms in which analogy questions are presented; various types of relationships; and an analysis of sample test questions.

Part Two, the major part of the book, is completely programmed with approximately 1400 frames (questions). These frames are presented in units, the first of which is "Relationships Illustrated." The latter is made up of fifteen different kinds of analogy relationships that commonly appear on analogy tests. Each relationship type is treated separately.

The second unit consists of several hundred analogy questions of "Miscellaneous Types"—that is, with no breakdown into the various kinds of relationships. On a regular test such as the Scholastic Aptitude Test or the Miller Analogy Test, analogies are presented in this potpourri manner.

The third unit is composed of 375 college entrance-type analogies.

The fourth unit of Part Two is made up of a Miller Analogy-type Test patterned closely after the actual Miller Analogy Test. Like the real test, this sample test consists of 100 analogy questions.

The fifth and final unit includes "Analogies Requiring a Good Vocabulary."

Part Three is made up of three Sample Miller Analogies Tests which have been patterned closely after the actual Miller Analogies Tests. An explanation of answers follows each of the three Sample Tests.

Part Four has four Nonverbal Analogy Tests. These will provide excellent practice for those taking an examination which includes the nonverbal reasoning type of question. Answers to these four tests are clearly explained.

PART ONE

Essential Information About Analogies

ANALOGY QUESTIONS

IN HIS CLASSIC textbook, *Principles of Psychology,* the great psychologist, William James, stated that "the faculty for perceiving analogies is the best indication of genius." He went on to say: "Some people are far more sensitive to resemblances, and far more ready to point out wherein they consist, than others are. They are the wits, the poets, the inventors, the scientific men, the practical genuises."

In referring to Newton and Darwin, two of the most famous scientists, James wrote: "The flash of similarity between an apple and the moon, between the rivalry for food in nature and the rivalry for man's selection, was too recondite to have occurred to any but exceptional minds. Genius, then . . . is identical with the possession of similar association to an extreme degree."

How to Use this Book

THIS BOOK WORKS like a teaching machine, without, however, employing the clumsy and expensive gadgetry often associated with these machines. You have here a programmed book —a book that is easy to use and effective in its teaching method.

First work with the *odd* pages only — page 1, 3, 5 . . . 105. Let us illustrate the method by turning to page 5. You will notice that there are 13 horizontal frames per page, alternately grey and white. The page is also divided, vertically, into a small column at the left and a large column at the right. The column at the left is the correct ANSWER column. We are now concerned with the right-hand column — the QUESTION column — Frame 3, the top frame:

Correct ANSWER
column

QUESTION
column

2. C	3. MELON is to RIND as ANIMAL is to (A) skin (B) horn (C) fox (D) cage

write *YOUR* answer **HERE**

In the box — FRAME 3 — you will see the analogy question, as above. There are four (sometimes five) answer choices: A, B, C, D, (E). In the space provided, write *YOUR* answer.

Now turn to the next odd page — page 7.

Still looking at the top frame, you will see that the CORRECT ANSWER to Frame 3 appears in the small left-hand column:

CORRECT
ANSWER-
(next QUESTION)

3. A	4. SHOE is to SHOELACE as DOOR is to (A) transom (B) threshold (C) hinge (D) key

The CORRECT answer to the Frame 3 question is A. Turn back to Frame 3 on page 5 and look at YOUR answer. If you did not answer the question correctly, study the question again until you understand it. Then cross out your incorrect answer and write the correct one. Now go on to Frame 4, page 7.

It is obvious, then, that you will always find the CORRECT ANSWER to a question by turning a page.

Go on in this manner, answering all the consecutively numbered questions in the top row, until you reach the last *odd* page, page 105. Then, return to page 1, this time answering all the questions in the *second* row. When you reach page 105, return again to page 1, and work on the *third* row of frames . . . and so on, until all questions on the right-hand (odd-numbered) pages have been answered.

Now start with page 2, a left-hand (even-numbered) page, and continue to answer all the questions on the left-hand pages — just as you did with the right-hand pages, above.

TESTS WHERE ANALOGIES ARE USED

A popular type of question that appears on various examinations is the ANALOGY QUESTION. Some of the vital tests in which the analogy question has an important place are the following:

SCHOLASTIC APTITUDE TEST

MILLER ANALOGY TEST

GRADUATE RECORD EXAMINATION

MEDICAL COLLEGE ADMISSION TEST

CIVIL SERVICE TESTS

WHAT THE ANALOGY QUESTION MEASURES

The analogy question tests your ability to see a relationship between words and to apply this relationship to other words. Although the verbal analogy test is, to some degree, an indicator of your vocabulary, it is essentially a test of your ability to think things out. In other words, analogy questions will spotlight your ability to think clearly — your ability to sidestep confusion of ideas. In mathematics, this type of situation is expressed as a proportion problem — for example, 3:5 :: 6:X. Verbal analogy questions, particularly the College Board type (see page 82), are written in this mathematical form.

THREE FORMS OF THE ANALOGY QUESTION

There are various forms of analogy questions. A frequent type is that in which two words which have some relationship to each other are presented. These two words are followed by a third word. The latter is related to one word in a group of choices in the same way that the first two words are related.

Type 1 - Example: WINTER is to SUMMER
as COLD is to
(A) wet (B) future (C) warm (D) freezing

WINTER and *SUMMER* bear an opposite relationship.
COLD and *WARM* have the same type of (opposite)
relationship. Therefore, (C) is the correct answer.

Another popular form of analogy is the type used on College Entrance Examinations. Each question consists, first, of two words which have some specific relationship to each other. Then, from four (or five) pairs of words which follow, you are to select the pair which is related in the same way as the words of the first pair are related to each other.

Type 2 - Example: SPELLING : PUNCTUATION ::
(A) pajamas : fatigue (B) powder : shaving
(C) bandage : cut (D) biology : physics

SPELLING and *PUNCTUATION* are elements of the
mechanics of English; *BIOLOGY* and *PHYSICS* are
two of the subjects that make up the field of science.
The other choices do not possess this PART : PART
relationship. Therefore, (D) is the correct choice.

Still another analogy form is that in which *one* of the four relationship elements is not specified. From choices offered — regardless of the position — you are to select the one choice which completes the relationship with the other three items.

Type 3 - Example: SUBMARINE : FISH as
(A) kite (B) limousine (C) feather (D) chirp :
BIRD

Both a *SUBMARINE* and a *FISH* are
found in the water; both a *KITE* and
BIRD are customarily seen in the air.
(A), consequently, is the correct answer.

This third type of analogy is used in the Miller Analogy Test, considered one of the most reliable and valid tests for selection of graduate students in universities, and high-level personnel in government, industry, and business.

TWO IMPORTANT STEPS TO ANALOGY SUCCESS

Step One—Determine the relationship between the first two words.

Step Two—Find the same relationship among the choices which follow the first two words.

NOW LET US APPLY THESE TWO STEPS

Directions: Each question consists of two words which have some relationship to each other. From the five following pairs of words, select the one which is related in the same way as the words of the first pair are related to each other:

ARC : CIRCLE :: (A) segment : cube (B) angle : triangle (C) tangent : circumference (D) circle : cube (E) cube : square

An arc is part of a circle, just as an angle is part of a triangle. The other choices do not bear this PART : WHOLE relationship. Therefore, (B) is correct

With the foregoing line of reasoning, you probably eliminated choice (A) immediately. Choice (B) seemed correct. Did you give it FINAL acceptance without considering the remaining choices? In this analogy question, choice (B), as it turned out, was the correct choice. However, let us change the question slightly:

ARC : CIRCLE :: (A) segment : cube (B) angle : triangle (C) tangent : circumference (D) circle : cube (E) line : square

Note that the (E) choice has been changed. (E) — not (B) — is now the correct answer. REASON: An arc is *any* part of the drawn circle. Likewise, a line is *any* part of the drawn square. However, an angle is *not* any part of the drawn triangle. The correct answer is, therefore, (E) line : square.

This illustration should caution you not to jump to conclusions. Consider *all* choices carefully before you reach your conclusion.

USE THE WORD THAT SHOWS THE RELATIONSHIP

The best way of determining the correct answer to an analogy question is to *provide the word or phrase* which shows the relationship that exists between the first two words. Let us illustrate with the following analogy question:

CLOCK : TIME :: (A) hour : latitude (B) thermometer : temperature (C) weather : climate (D) tide : moon

The problem is to determine which choice has the same relationship that *clock* has to *time*. Let us, now, provide the word or phrase which shows the relationship between *clock* and *time*. The word is *measures*. Choice B, then, is the correct answer since a thermometer *measures* temperature.

You will find that many of the choices which you are given to select from, have some relationship to the opening pair. You must be sure to select *that* choice which bears a relationship most closely approximating the relationship between the opening two words. See Note 2 on page xii.

KINDS OF RELATIONSHIP

In analogy questions, the relationship between the first two words may be one of several kinds. Following are relationship possibilities.

1. *Purpose Relationship*
   GLOVE : BALL :: (A) hook : fish (B) winter : weather (C) game : pennant (D) stadium : seats

2. *Cause and Effect Relationship*
   RACE : FATIGUE :: (A) track : athlete (B) ant : bug (C) fast : hunger (D) walking : running

3. *Part : Whole Relationship*
   SNAKE : REPTILE :: (A) patch : thread (B) removal : snow (C) struggle : wrestle (D) hand : clock

4. *Part : Part Relationship*
   GILL : FIN :: (A) tube : antenna (B) instrument : violin (C) sea : fish (D) salad : supper

5. *Action to Object Relationship*
   KICK : FOOTBALL :: (A) kill : bomb (B) break : pieces (C) question : team (D) smoke : pipe

6. *Object to Action Relationship*
   STEAK : BROIL :: (A) bread : bake (B) food : sell (C) wine : pour (D) sugar : spill

7. *Synonym Relationship*
   ENORMOUS : HUGE :: (A) rogue : rock (B) muddy : unclear (C) purse : kitchen (D) black : white

8. *Antonym Relationship*
   PURITY : EVIL :: (A) suavity : bluntness (B) north : climate (C) angel : horns (D) boldnes : victory

9. *Place Relationship*
   MIAMI : FLORIDA :: (A) Chicago : United States (B) New York : Albany
   (C) United States : Chicago (D) Albany : New York

10. *Degree Relationship*
    WARM : HOT :: (A) glue : paste (B) climate : weather
    (C) fried egg : boiled egg (D) bright : genius

11. *Characteristic Relationship*
    IGNORANCE : POVERTY :: (A) blood : wound (B) money : dollar
    (C) schools : elevators (D) education : stupidity

12. *Sequence Relationship*
    SPRING : SUMMER :: (A) Thursday : Wednesday (B) Wednesday : Monday
    (C) Monday : Wednesday (D) Wednesday : Thursday

13. *Grammatical Relationship*
    RESTORE : CLIMB :: (A) segregation : seem (B) into : nymph
    (C) tearoom : although (D) overpower : seethe

14. *Numerical Relationship*
    4 : 12 :: (A) 10 : 16 (B) 9 : 27 (C) 3 : 4 (D) 12 : 6

15. *Association Relationship*
    DEVIL : WRONG :: (A) color : sidewalk (B) slipper : state (C) ink : writing
    (D) picture : bed

Answers to Above Analogy Questions

1. A	3. D	5. D	7. B	9. D	11. A	13. D	15. C
2. C	4. A	6. A	8. A	10. D	12. D	14. B	

Note 1: In many analogy questions, the incorrect choices may relate in some way to the first two words. Don't let this association mislead you. For example, in Number 4 above (PART: PART RELATIONSHIP example), the correct answer is (A) tube : antenna. The choice (C) sea : fish is incorrect, although these two latter words are associated in a general sense with the first two words (gill : fin).

Note 2: Very often, the relationship of the first two words may apply to more than *one* of the choices given. In such a case, you must narrow down the initial relationship in order to get the correct choice. For example, in Number 6 above (OBJECT TO ACTION RELATIONSHIP), a STEAK is something that you B R O I L. Now let us consider the choices: BREAD is something that you BAKE; FOOD is something that you SELL; WINE is something that you POUR; and SUGAR is something that you (can) SPILL. Thus far, each choice seems correct. Let us now narrow down the relationship: a STEAK is something that you BROIL with *heat*. The only choice that fulfills this *complete* relationship is (A) BREAD—something that you BAKE with *heat*. It follows that (A) is the correct choice.

SAMPLE TEST QUESTIONS ANALYZED

We have seen that there are numerous types of analogy relationships (page xi). However, if you follow the procedures indicated in the analysis of the sample questions (below), you will be able to determine, in a similar manner, the various relationships in practically all of the analogy questions you will get on an actual test. If you proceed on your actual test as we suggest below, you will raise your mark considerably.

The important thing to remember in answering an analogy question is to determine the *specific relationship* of the first two words of the analogy — then make that choice which bears a similar relationship.

Analysis No. 1

CUP is to DRINK as PLATE is to
    (A) supper   (B) fork
    (C) dine   (D) earthenware
              (E) silver

1. What is the relationship between CUP (noun) and DRINK (verb)?

2. It is obvious that one drinks *from* a cup.

3. What does one do *from* a plate in the same manner that one drinks from a cup?

4. It becomes apparent that of the five choices offered, (C) dine, is the only one which bears a similar relationship, since one DINES from a PLATE.

5. A closer analogy would have been "one EATS from a plate," but since this word is not offered, the *best* of the five choices is "DINE."

6. Notice that *all* of the remaining choices bear *some* relationship to the word PLATE but *not* the same that CUP bears to DRINK.

    a) "Supper" is related to "plate" since one's supper may be eaten from a plate. Supper, however, is a *noun*, and the part of speech required is a *verb*.

    b) "Fork" is related to "plate" since in one sense they are synonyms. There the relationship required, so it must be eliminated.

    d) "Earthenware" is related to "plate" since many plates are made of earthenware, but this also is not the relationship called for.

    e) "Silver" is related to "plate" since in one sense they are synonymous. There is also a relationship established in the word "silver-plated," but neither of these is the relationship required.

Analysis No. 2

GUILLOTINE is to DECAPITATE as RAZOR is to
(A) beard   (B) hair
(C) shave   (D) cut
        (E) steel

This is the type of analogy which deals with the use, purpose or function of an object or instrument.

1. The purpose of a "guillotine" is to "decapitate."

2. What is a "razor" used for?

3. It is obvious that the most important use of the razor is "to shave," so (C) is the correct answer.

4. Notice the relationships of the remaining choices:

   a) "Razor" is related to "beard," since it is used to cut beards, but it is not the relationship required. Also, the sense of the analogy calls for a verb, *not* a noun.

   b) "Razor" is related to "hair," since it cuts hair, but "hair" is not the purpose of "razor."

   d) "Cut" is one of the uses of a razor, but it is not its primary function. Relatively it is not as important as "shave."

   e) "Steel" is related to "razor" in the sense that some razors are made of steel, but since "steel" is not the function of a razor, it must be eliminated as incorrect.

Analysis No. 3

ADDER is to SNAKE as CROCODILE is to
(A) ruminant   (B) marsh
(C) reptile   (D) carnivore
        (E) rapacious

This is a type of analogy question frequently met on examinations. The candidate must learn to distinguish between that which is specific and that which is general. In many cases it is a question of allocating a species of an animal, plant, tree, bird, etc. in its broader classification.

1. An "adder" is a "kind" or "type" of snake.

2. "Snake" is a general term including many different species, of which "adder" is only one.

3. In the same way, which of the five choices is the general classification under which the specie "crocodile" can be classified?

a) A "ruminant" is "an animal that chews the cud," as a goat or a sheep. A crocodile is *not* a ruminant.

b) A "marsh" is a tract of low, miry land. It has no connection with types of crocodiles.

c) "Reptile" is a broad classification of animals including the crocodile. It has the same relationship to "crocodile" as "adder" has to "snake," and is, therefore, the correct choice.

d) A "carnivore" is a mammalian animal which lives on flesh for food. The crocodile is not of this type.

e) "Rapacious" is an adjective meaning "subsisting on prey or animals seized by violence." Since "rapacious" is not a type of crocodile, it could not possibly be the correct choice.

Analysis No. 4

BREAKABLE is to FRANGIBLE as GULLIBLE is to

    (A) credulous   (B) deceptive

    (C) capable   (D) lurid

          (E) marine

1. This is an analogy formed by comparing two adjectives.

2. They are synonymous since they have the same meanings.

3. Inasmuch as the first two words of the analogy are adjectives, the second pair must also be adjectives.

4. "Gullible" is an exact synonym of "credulous" and is therefore the most correct choice.

5. None of the other choices bears any resemblance in meaning to "gullible."

2

PART TWO

Programmed Analogy Questions

Practice Using Answer Sheets

SAMPLE		SCORES	
I. CHICAGO is		1 _____	5 _____
I-1 a country	I-4 a city	2 _____	6 _____
I-2 a mountain	I-5 a state	3 _____	7 _____
I-3 an island		4 _____	8 _____

Sample answer row: 1 2 3 4 5 — space 4 blackened.

Answer grid (each item has columns: T a, F b, c, d, e):

1, 2, 3, 4
5, 6, 7, 8
9, 10, 11, 12
13, 14, 15, 16
17, 18, 19, 20
21, 22, 23, 24
25, 26, 27, 28
29, 30, 31, 32
33, 34, 35, 36
37, 38, 39, 40
41, 42, 43, 44
45, 46, 47, 48
49, 50, 51, 52
53, 54, 55, 56
57, 58, 59, 60
61, 62, 63, 64
65, 66, 67, 68
69, 70, 71, 72
73, 74, 75, 76
77, 78, 79, 80
81, 82, 83, 84
85, 86, 87, 88
89, 90, 91, 92
93, 94, 95, 96
97, 98, 99, 100
101, 102, 103, 104
105, 106, 107, 108
109, 110, 111, 112
113, 114, 115, 116
117, 118, 119, 120
121, 122, 123, 124
125, 126, 127, 128
129, 130, 131, 132
133, 134, 135, 136
137, 138, 139, 140
141, 142, 143, 144
145, 146, 147, 148
149, 150

---

54.   HORSE is to RIDER
as ENGINE is to
(A) passenger (B) engineer (C) train (D) coal

106.
B

107.   FLY is to SPIDER
as MOUSE is to
(A) rat (B) cat (C) rodent (D) animal

159.
B

160.   MIDDLE AGES is to RENAISSANCE
as 1700 is to
(A) Dark Ages (B) 1500 (C) Ancient Greece (D) 20th Century

212.
C

213.   SHIP is to CHRISTEN
as MONUMENT is to
(A) revere (B) hail (C) sculpture (D) dedicate

265.
A

266.   LOUD is to THUNDER
as LARGE is to
(A) monkey (B) midget (C) whale (D) blatancy

318.
C

319.   CRATER is to VOLCANO
as CHIMNEY is to
(A) fire (B) house (C) fuel (D) smoke

371.
C

372.   PETAL is to FLOWER
as FUR is to
(A) coat (B) rabbit (C) warm (D) women

424.
A

425.   TONE is to HEARING
as COLOR is to
(A) pigment (B) sight (C) melody (D) picture

477.
C

478.   VALOR is to COWARDICE
as WHITE is to
(A) color (B) yellow (C) pigment (D) black

530.
B

531.   RICE is to CEREAL
as APPLE is to
(A) pear (B) peel (C) fruit (D) box

583.
D

584.   ATOM is to MOLECULE
as POUND is to
(A) quart (B) pound (C) package (D) ton

636.
C

637.   WEEK is to DAY
as DAY is to
(A) month (B) second (C) hour (D) night

---

689. D	690. ACUTE is to CHRONIC TURN TO PAGE 4 TOP FRAME (FRAME 691) as TEMPORARY is to (A) sardonic (B) tonic (C) persistent (D) pretty (E) sick
742. E	743. GUN is to HOLSTER as SWORD is to (A) pistol (B) scabbard (C) warrior (D) slay (E) plunder
795. D	796. CAMPHOR is to AROMATIC as LILAC is to (A) lavender (B) flower (C) fragrant (D) rose (E) sentimental
848. A	849. CONDONE : OFFENSE :: (A) punish : criminal (B) mitigate : penitence (C) overlook : aberration (D) mistake : judgment (E) ignore : loyalty
901. D	902. PROTOPLASM : CELL :: (A) chain : link (B) fibre : plastic (C) coin : money (D) chemistry : elements (E) food : wheat
954. C	955. CORRUGATED : STRIPED :: (A) box : zebra (B) paint : crayon (C) roughness : smoothness (D) pit : dot
1007. C	1008. DESTRUCTION : DEATH :: (A) wash : dirt (B) germs : infection (C) sneeze : cold (D) cough : sneeze
1060. D	1061. OXYGEN : GASEOUS :: (A) feather : light (B) mercury : fluid (C) iron : heavy (D) sand : grainy
1113. C	1114. AGILE : ACROBAT :: (A) grease : mechanic (B) peanuts : vendor (C) plant : fruit (D) eloquent : orator
1166. C	1167. CAT : MOUSE :: (A) bird : worm (B) dog : tail (C) trap : cheese (D) hide : seek
1219. C	1220. REMBRANDT : (A) Herodotus (B) Titian (C) Socrates (D) Bacon as PICASSO : GAUGIN
1272. D	1273. (A) Thomas (B) Jack (C) Oscar (D) William : ACTOR as PENNANT : TEAM
1325. C	1326. ARROGATE is to USURP as CLOY is to (A) collect (B) employ (C) glut (D) cut

2. NOSE is to SMELL
as TEETH is to
(A) see (B) dentist (C) chew (D) toothpaste

TURN TO PAGE 5
TOP FRAME (FRAME 3)

54. B	55. NET is to FISHERMAN as GUN is to (A) bullet (B) deer (C) policeman (D) hunter
107. B	108. WEAK is to STRONG as UNABLE is to (A) clumsy (B) cowardly (C) able (D) failure
160. D	161. M. GRAMMATICAL RELATIONSHIP (Frames 162-167)
213. D	214. HORSE is to HAIR as MAN is to (A) woman (B) whip (C) clothes (D) tie
266. C	267. DISTRACTING is to NOISE as SOOTHING is to (A) medicine (B) music (C) bleeding (D) opera
319. B	320. AIR is to SUFFOCATION as FOOD is to (A) starvation (B) indigestion (C) energy (D) life
372. B	373. PLAYER is to TEAM as EAR is to (A) face (B) body (C) head (D) brain
425. B	426. EDUCATED is to KNOW as RICH is to (A) poor (B) own (C) wise (D) intelligent
478. D	479. CALF is to COW as CUB is to (A) scout (B) bear (C) baby (D) woods
531. C	532. INCLEMENT is to CLEAR as PERTINENT is to (A) pert (B) cloudy (C) irrelevant (D) perceptive
584. D	585. RESEARCH is to DISCOVERY as PRAYER is to (A) church (B) bible (C) religion (D) fulfilment
637. C	638. CALF is to SHOE as GOOSE is to (A) feature (B) gander (C) geese (D) pillow

690. C	691. VALLEY is to GORGE TURN TO PAGE 6 TOP FRAME (FRAME 692) as MOUNTAIN is to (A) hill (B) cliff (C) pinnacle (D) high (E) altitude
743. B	744. NECKLACE is to PEARLS as CHAIN is to (A) metal (B) prisoner (C) locket (D) silver (E) links
796. C	797. PUNGENT is to ODOR as SHRILL is to (A) whisper (B) piercing (C) shriek (D) depth (E) sound
849. A	850. POWER : BATTERY :: (A) vitamins : metabolism (B) recuperation : convalescence (C) exercise : strength (D) automobile : engine (E) light : kerosene
902. A	903. MACAROON : ALMOND :: (A) bread : dough (B) mint : flavor (C) vanilla : bean (D) caramel : butter (E) bread : wheat
955. D	956. ENERGY : DISSIPATE :: (A) battery : recharge (B) atom : split (C) food : heat (D) money : squander
1008. B	1009. EYE : FACE :: (A) ring : finger (B) stem : root (C) knob : door (D) shoe : foot
1061. B	1062. ROD : FEET :: (A) pound : ounce (B) inch : yard (C) pint : quart (D) minute : second
1114. D	1115. KNOWLEDGE : WISDOM :: (A) glue : paste (B) disease : filth (C) heat : climate (D) climate : weather
1167. A	1168. WING : BEAK :: (A) button : shirt (B) Pluto : Venus (C) house : chimney (D) bird : cage
1220. B	1221. (A) history (B) calculus (C) economics (D) grammar : MATHEMATICS as ICHTHYOLOGY : ZOOLOGY
1273. C	1274. STRABISMUS : ASTIGMATISM as MALOCCLUSION : (A) headache (B) caries (C) malformation (D) dandruff
1326. C	1327. DENIGRATE is to DEFAMER as MEDIATE is to (A) mathematician (B) arbitrator (C) employer (D) laborer

2. **C**	**3.** MELON is to RIND as ANIMAL is to (A) skin (B) horn (C) fox (D) cage

TURN TO PAGE 7
TOP FRAME (FRAME 4)

55. **D**

56. HEAR is to SOUND
as SEE is to
(A) move (B) taste (C) picture (D) vision

108. **C**

109. SUMMER is to WINTER
as EVENING is to
(A) sunset (B) coolness (C) morning (D) darkness

162. WRING is to WRUNG
as LIE is to
(A) lie (B) laid (C) lies (D) lay

214. **C**

215. YEAR is to CALENDAR
as DAY is to
(A) decade (B) clock (C) minute (D) month

267. **B**

268. GRASS is to GREEN
as BLUE is to
(A) star (B) sky (C) flag (D) leaf

320. **A**

321. FATHER is to BROTHER
as MOTHER is to
(A) daughter (B) sister (C) aunt (D) niece

373. **C**

374. TOE is to FOOT
as HEAD is to
(A) ear (B) arm (C) body (D) nose

426. **B**

427. WORDS is to BOOK
as NOTES is to
(A) piano (B) song (C) sculpture (D) fragrance

479. **B**

480. SKY is to GROUND
as CEILING is to
(A) plaster (B) roof (C) top (D) floor

532. **C**

533. FOOD is to NUTRITION
as LIGHT is to
(A) vision (B) bulb (C) electricity (D) watt

585. **D**

586. PRESENT is to BIRTHDAY
as REWARD is to
(A) accomplishment (B) punishment (C) medal (D) money

638. **D**

639. FISH is to FINS
as BIRD is to
(A) fly (B) feather (C) wings (D) pigeon

691. B	692. GASOLINE is to PETROLEUM as SUGAR is to (A) oil (B) cane (C) plant (D) molasses (E) sweet	TURN TO PAGE 8 TOP FRAME (FRAME 693)
744. E	745. VALISE is to LEATHER as HIGHWAY is to (A) passage (B) road (C) asphalt (D) trail (E) journey	
797. E	798. MOUSE is to RODENT as WHALE is to (A) animal (B) ocean (C) gigantic (D) mammal (E) spawn	
850. E	851. DEPRESSION : UNEMPLOYMENT :: (A) legislation : lobbying (B) emaciation : debilitation (C) capital : interest (D) deterioriation : rust (E) recession : inefficiency	
903. D	904. INTEGER : DECIMAL :: (A) 100 : 10 (B) 1 : 0 (C) decimal : fraction (D) whole number : fraction (E) 100 : per cent	
956. D	957. ICING : CAKE :: (A) veneer : table (B) frost : lake (C) pastry : bakery (D) slicing : rake	
1009. C	1010. CHALK : BLACKBOARD :: (A) door : handle (B) table : chair (C) ink : paper (D) dog : tail	
1062. B	1063. THROW : BALL :: (A) shoot : trigger (B) pat : dog (C) mew : cat (D) boil : shell	
1115. B	1116. YELL : UTTER :: (A) scream : deafen (B) shout : call (C) child : infant (D) bend : break	
1168. B	1169. SWEATER : WARMTH :: (A) wool : cotton (B) glamor : beauty (C) food : nourishment (D) table : comfort	
1221. B	1222. (A) champagne (B) pipe (C) child (D) name : BUBBLE as SANDWICH : HAM	
1274. B	1275. MIDAS : BRYAN as GOLD : (A) silver (B) politician (C) miser (D) men	
1327. B	1328. INCHOATE is to TERMINAL as SATURNINE is to (A) mercurial (B) planetary (C) saturated (D) relaxed	

3. A	4. SHOE is to SHOELACE as DOOR is to (A) transom (B) threshold (C) hinge (D) key
56. C	57. OBEY is to CHILDREN as COMMAND is to (A) performance (B) parents (C) army (D) result
109. C	110. RIGHT is to LEFT as LOW is to (A) bottom (B) high (C) sorrow (D) note
162. D	163. ROSE is to RISE as WENT is to (A) going (B) gone (C) go (D) return
215. B	216. SUCCEED is to FAIL as PROPER is to (A) incorrect (B) proposed (C) propped (D) fatherly
268. B	269. TODAY is to YESTERDAY as PRESENT is to (A) yesterday (B) Monday (C) past (D) gift
321. B	322. WATER is to IRRIGATION as AIR is to (A) oxygen (B) respiration (C) ventilation (D) atmosphere
374. C	375. NAIL is to FINGER as TOE is to (A) shoe (B) foot (C) sock (D) leg
427. B	428. PIPE is to PLUMBER as BOARD is to (A) mechanic (B) propeller (C) carpenter (D) lacquer
480. D	481. WATER is to AIR as BOAT is to (A) sail (B) sea (C) yacht (D) airplane
533. A	534. BRIEF is to BOMBASTIC as LAX is to (A) stringent (B) medicinal (C) fishy (D) filthy
586. A	587. WARLIKE is to PEACEFUL as MARTIAL is to (A) military (B) noisy (C) worried (D) halcyon
639. C	640. DEAFNESS is to TONE as BLINDNESS is to (A) sight (B) color (C) lightness (D) vision

692. B	693. MONARCHY is to KING as DEMOCRACY is to (A) vote (B) freedom (C) people (D) republic (E) congress
745. C	746. SERFDOM is to FEUDALISM as ENTREPRENEUR is to (A) laissez faire (B) captain (C) radical (D) agriculture (E) capitalism
798. D	799. PROSTRATE is to FLAT as VERTICAL is to (A) circular (B) plumb (C) horizontal (D) inclined (E) geometric
851. D	852. DIETING : OVERWEIGHT :: (A) overeating : gluttony (B) gourmet : underweight (C) poverty : sickness (D) doctor : arthritis (E) resting : fatigue
904. D	905. HOUSE : MORTGAGE:: (A) car : lien (B) inventory : merchandise (C) word : promise (D) security : price (E) equity : interest
957. A	958. MONEY : EMBEZZLEMENT :: (A) bank : cashier (B) passage : plagiarism (C) remarks : insult (D) radiation : bomb
1010. C	1011. FOIL : FENCE :: (A) pencil : pen (B) candle : heat (C) train : travel (D) sleep : bed
1063. B	1064. CLIMB : TREE :: (A) row : canoe (B) shoe : horse (C) throw : balloon (D) file : finger
1116. B	1117. LION : CUB:: (A) mother : aunt (B) aunt : child (C) mother : child (D) father : grandfather
1169. C	1170. DIET : WEIGHT :: (A) food : fat (B) dinner : supper (C) bread : starchy (D) drug : pain
1222. B	1223. RAM : (A) duck (B) ewe (C) slam (D) butt as COCK : HEN
1275. A	1276. (A) Sinatra (B) Como (C) Caruso (D) Barrymore : CHALIAPIN as TOSCANINI : STOKOWSKI
1328. A	1329. LITTORAL is to COAST as PECTORAL is to (A) throat (B) leg (C) skeleton (D) chest

4. D	5. GAS is to CAR as WOOD is to (A) tree (B) fire (C) stove (D) bench
57. B	58. BARK is to DOG as ROAR is to (A) lion (B) snake (C) lamb (D) train
110. B	111. ENEMIES is to FRIENDS as DESPISE is to (A) hate (B) pacify (C) reconcile (D) esteem
163. C	164. SHABBY is to SHABBILY as HARMONIOUS is to (A) harp (B) harmonica (C) harmoniously (D) harmony
216. A	217. INTELLIGENCE is to IDIOT as WEALTH is to (A) money (B) poverty (C) millionaire (D) pauper
269. C	270. BLACK is to WHITE as NIGHT is to (A) stillness (B) sun (C) moon (D) day
322. C	323. GLORY is to SHAME as VICTORY is to (A) defeat (B) winner (C) reward (D) conqueror
375. B	376. SUNDER is to CONSOLIDATE as TANGIBLE is to (A) abstract (B) tasty (C) possible (D) tangled
428. C	429. WIRE is to ELECTRICITY as PIPE is to (A) power (B) fervid (C) gas (D) water
481. D	482. RETREAT is to ADVANCE as TIMID is to (A) cowardly (B) bold (C) fearful (D) shy
534. A	535. ATTORNEY is to TRIAL as SURGEON is to (A) doctor (B) patient (C) operation (D) ether
587. D	588. INCIPIENT is to TERMINAL as SALUTATORIAN is to (A) valedictorian (B) graduate (C) diploma (D) college
640. B	641. SATIN is to GINGHAM as PLATINUM is to (A) gold (B) lead (C) diamond (D) brilliant

693. C	694. LATITUDE is to LONGITUDE as WARP is to (A) weave (B) woof (C) thread (D) line (E) straight
746. E	747. FIN is to FISH as PROPELLER is to (A) auto (B) airplane (C) grain elevator (D) water (E) bus
799. B	800. STRAND is to BEACH as STRAIN is to (A) tension (B) torture (C) isthmus (D) relieve (E) heritage
852. E	853. STREPTOCOCCI : PNEUMONIA :: (A) boat : trip (B) quinine : malaria (C) cause : sickness (D) malnutrition : berri berri (E) medicine : sickness
905. A	906. HYGROMETER : BAROMETER :: (A) water : mercury (B) snow : rain (C) humidity : pressure (D) temperature : weather (E) forecast : rain
958. B	959. CORRESPONDENCE : CLERK :: (A) office : manager (B) secretary : stenographer (C) orders : accountant (D) records : archivist
1011. C	1012. FRAME : PICTURE :: (A) cup : saucer (B) table : floor (C) radio : sound (D) cover : book
1064. B	1065. ROOM : HOUSE :: (A) refrigerator : kitchen (B) chair : room (C) roof : building (D) wheel : chair
1117. C	1118. BACTERIA : ILLNESS :: (A) medicine: bacteria (B) illness : health (C) bomb : explosion (D) solid : liquid
1170. D	1171. PLASTER : MORTAR :: (A) brush : paint (B) drink : soda (C) sweep : broom (D) blow : bubble
1223. B	1224. NOVEL: (A) epic (B) volume (C) words (D) story as TOM SAWYER : AENEID
1276. C	1277. MISSHAPEN : TISSUE as (A) cannon (B) cleaner (C) fissure (C) appearance : MISSILE
1329. D	1330. BUCOLIC is to PEACE as CIMMERIAN is to (A) warlike (B) tenebrous (C) doubtful (D) smirking

5. B	6. RING is to FINGER as SHOE is to (A) cobbler (B) lace (C) store (D) foot
58. A	59. ACT is to ACTRESS as SONG is to (A) songstress (B) singing (C) chorus (D) music
111. D	112. BLAME is to PRAISE as FAIL is to (A) succeed (B) emerge (C) defeat (D) condemn
164. C	165. PLAUSIBILITY is to PLAUSIBLE as INFAMY is to (A) infamous (B) inflammatory (C) infernal (D) unfamiliar
217. D	218. WARDEN is to GUARD as DOCTOR is to (A) nurse (B) patient (C) surgeon (D) ward
270. D	271. WALKS is to MAN as SWIMS is to (A) fish (B) pool (C) pier (D) boar
323. A	324. RIVALS is to OPPOSITION as TEAM is to (A) argument (B) harmony (C) group (D) togetherness
376. A	377. HORSE is to HERD as MOUNTAIN is to (A) volcano (B) rock (C) hill (D) range
429. C	430. IDLE is to LAZY as BUSY is to (A) exuberant (B) ambitious (C) lassitude (D) beaver
482. B	483. JOY is to SORROW as LAUGHTER is to (A) joke (B) fun (C) tears (D) ridicule
535. C	536. SEEK is to AVOID as INDULGE is to (A) pursue (B) abstain (C) hunt (D) find
588. A	589. STATUE is to SCULPTOR as VERSE is to (A) book (B) rhythm (C) poet (D) symbol
641. B	642. PESTILENCE is to DEATH as WAR is to (A) devastation (B) victory (C) peace (D) defense

694. B	695. ELEGANCE is to LUXURY as POVERTY is to (A) penury (B) misery (C) poorhouse (D) hunger (E) paucity
747. B	748. PULP is to PAPER as HEMP is to (A) rope (B) baskets (C) yarn (D) cotton (E) silk
800. A	801. DIGITALIS is to STIMULANT as SENNA is to (A) peroxide (B) cathartic (C) flower (D) rust (E) tea
853. D	854. NAIVE : CHEAT :: (A) sensible : succeed (B) contentious : scorn (C) gullible : convince (D) hurt : retaliate (E) simple : win
906. C	907. NEGOTIABLE : CHECK :: (A) frozen : asset (B) inventory : merchandise (C) bank : money (D) trade : tariff (E) flowing : river
959. D	960. PROJECTILE : TRAJECTORY :: (A) satellite : orbit (B) bullet : weapon (C) project : tragedy (D) rejection : renunciation
1012. D	1013. SHOVEL : HOE :: (A) eraser : chalk (B) garden : gardener (C) farm : house (D) house : lawn
1065. C	1066. BLISTER : SKIN :: (A) sore : toe (B) ball : pitcher (C) sty : eye (D) store : street
1118. C	1119. 20 : 21 :: (A) 5 : 10 (B) A : B (C) 10 : 9 (D) S : V
1171. C	1172. VANDAL : CONTEMPT :: (A) sculptor : talent (B) elastic : tension (C) philanthropist : charity (D) wood : strength
1224. A	1225. ONOMATOPOEIA : (A) potato (B) touch (C) saying (D) sound as METAPHOR : COMPARISON
1277. C	1278. TIGER : MAN as (A) fish (B) school (C) shark (D) whale : LION
1330. B	1331. LIMPID is to LUCID as TURBID is to (A) torpid (B) muddy (C) truculent (D) urban

6. D	7. SCISSORS is to CUT as PEN is to (A) point (B) ink (C) pig (D) write
59. A	60. SCRUB is to FLOOR as SCOUR is to (A) sweep (B) pan (C) kitchen (D) cleanse
112. A	113. SCINTILLATING is to VAPID as BRAVERY is to (A) home (B) cowardice (C) Indian (D) warrior
165. A	166. COCKROACH is to PLUM as CHICKEN is to (A) victory (B) sadness (C) wolf (D) justice
218. A	219. CALM is to STORM as PEACE is to (A) stillness (B) war (C) disturbance (D) anger
271. A	272. HEIGHT is to ALTITUDE as PIT is to (A) abyss (B) date (C) coal (D) darkness
324. B	325. COLLAR is to NECK as BELT is to (A) body (B) buckle (C) waist (D) fastener
377. D	378. SHEEP is to FLOCK as BOAT is to (A) crew (B) ocean (C) captain (D) fleet
430. B	431. POLISH is to MANICURIST as POLISH is to (A) bootblack (B) shoe (C) buff (D) pedicurist
483. C	484. SINKS is to ROCK as FLOATS is to (A) feather (B) light (C) flies (D) drowns
536. B	537. PLAY is to AUDIENCE as BOOK is to (A) writer (B) publisher (C) plot (D) reader
589. C	590. RECOUNT is to DISCOUNT as COIFFURE is to (A) care (B) hair (C) impure (D) beauty
642. A	643. CAT is to MOUSE as WOLF is to (A) fox (B) chicken (C) sheep (D) vulture

695. A	696. ARTIFICE is to FINESSE as INEPT is to (A) inefficient (B) artistic (C) tricky (D) insatiable (E) clever
748. A	749. SKIN is to MAN as HIDE is to (A) scales (B) fur (C) animal (D) hair (E) fish
801. B	802. STREW is to DISPERSE as STRAY is to (A) deviate (B) utter (C) dredge (D) relegate (E) annex
854. C	855. ERRORS : INEXPERIENCE :: (A) skill : mistakes (B) training : economy (C) success : victory (D) news : publication (E) thefts : carelessness
907. E	908. CAUCASIAN : SAXON :: (A) white : colored (B) Chinese : Indian (C) furniture : chair (D) carriage : horse (E) city : house
960. A	961. CLOTH : TEXTURE :: (A) wool : silk (B) book : text (C) wood : grain (D) linen : flax
1013. A	1014. CHILD : FAMILY :: (A) bird : nest (B) mother : baby (C) tentacle : octopus (D) flower : tulip
1066. C	1067. EXPLOSION : DEBRIS :: (A) train : car (B) bruise : fall (C) television : dial (D) locusts : holocaust
1119. B	1120. SORROW : DEATH :: (A) laugh : cry (B) plum : peach (C) happiness : birth (D) fear : hate
1172. C	1173. TEPID : HOT :: (A) pat : slap (B) winter : summer (C) topple : tumble (D) bing : bang
1225. D	1226. CAESAR : HORACE as PERICLES : (A) Moses (B) Plato (C) Erasmus (D) Paul
1278. D	1279. CIRCLE : OVAL as PARALLELOGRAM : (A) figure (B) octagon (C) starfish (D) semicircle
1331. B	1332. PHYSIOGNOMY is to FACE as NECROLOGY is to (A) philosophy (B) magic (C) psychology (D) mortality

7. **D**	**8.** REFRIGERATOR is to MEAT as BANK is to (A) cashier (B) combination (C) money (D) watchman
60. **B**	**61.** PEEL is to BANANA as SHELL is to (A) sea (B) fish (C) sand (D) oyster
113. **B**	**114.** I. PLACE RELATIONSHIP (Frames 115-131)
166. **C**	**167.** ITS is to BABIES' as THEIR is to (A) you (B) your (C) ladies (D) we
219. **B**	**220.** WOOD is to DECAY as IRON is to (A) dampness (B) rust (C) steel (D) ore
272. **A**	**273.** WORST is to WORSE as WORSE is to (A) bad (B) good (C) best (D) better
325. **C**	**326.** TYRANNY is to DEMOCRACY as CONSERVATIVE is to (A) Republican (B) conserving (C) religious (D) radical
378. **D**	**379.** FINGER is to HAND as HAIR is to (A) barber (B) baldness (C) scalp (D) blonde
431. **A**	**432.** BIRDS is to FEATHERS as FISH is to (A) fins (B) claws (C) gills (D) scales
484. **A**	**485.** FUR is to SQUIRREL as FEATHER is to (A) hat (B) tickle (C) light (D) bird
537. **D**	**538.** PARACHUTE is to PLANE as LIFE PRESERVER is to (A) fish (B) boat (C) water (D) chest
590. **C**	**591.** MASCULINE is to MAN as FEMININE is to (A) child (B) woman (C) gender (D) person
643. **C**	**644.** NAPKIN is to HEM as WHEEL is to (A) turn (B) rim (C) spoke (D) wagon

696. A	697. EWE is to RAM as MARE is to (A) cow (B) antelope (C) calf (D) stallion (E) fawn
749. C	750. RAIN is to DROP as SNOW is to (A) ice (B) cold (C) zero (D) flake (E) hail
802. A	803. PRECARIOUS is to CERTAIN as ZEALOUS is to (A) apathetic (B) ardent (C) indigent (D) sensitive (E) enervating
855. E	856. FORECAST : HAPPENING :: (A) prophesy : miracle (B) analyze : problem (C) forestall : disaster (D) exculpate : criminal (E) elucidate : explanation
908. C	909. OCTAVO : BINDING :: (A) pica : printing (B) music : octave (C) day : week (D) pamphlet : book (E) ruler : artist
961. C	962. GOVERNMENT : EXILE (A) police : arrest (B) judge : convict (C) constitution : amendment (D) church : excommunicate
1014. C	1015. .001 : .000001 :: (A) 2 : 4 (B) 1/4 : 1/8 (C) 1/4 : 16 (D) 4 : 1/16
1067. D	1068. PEDAL : BICYCLE :: (A) run : race (B) climb : hill (C) wind : clock (D) switch : motor
1120. C	1121. GOSSIP : EXAGGERATION :: (A) smoke : fire (B) cat : chat (C) boy : brother (D) climb : cry
1173. A	1174. WAR : DEFEAT :: (A) arm : leg (B) contest : victory (C) crime : praise (D) doctor : lawyer
1226. B	1227. LEMON : MERINGUE as (A) pineapple (B) wood (C) goat (D) vegetable : CHEESE
1279. B	1280. NEGRO : QUADROON as (A) Japanese (B) Chinese (C) Oriental (D) Asian : NISEI
1332. D	1333. ARCHAEOLOGIST is to ANTIQUITY as ICHTHYOLOGIST is to (A) theology (B) marine life (C) horticulture (D) mysticism

8. C	9. HAND is to GLOVE as HEAD is to (A) hat (B) warmth (C) earmuffs (D) hair
61. D	62. BEHEAD is to GUILLOTINE as HANG is to (A) gallows (B) nail (C) murderer (D) picture
	115. THIMBLE is to FINGER as SOCK is to (A) band (B) felt (C) hat rack (D) foot
167. B	168. **N. NUMERICAL RELATIONSHIP** (Frames 169-174)
220. B	221. ICE is to SKATE as WATER is to (A) swim (B) distill (C) rain (D) sport
273. A	274. TREE is to ELM as FLOWER is to (A) garden (B) hothouse (C) rose (D) spade
326. D	327. STATION is to TRAIN as WHARF is to (A) steamer (B) pier (C) water (D) river
379. C	380. PART is to WHOLE as SPOKE is to (A) bicycle (B) tire (C) wheel (D) rubber
432. A	433. FACT is to SCIENCE as IDEA is to (A) philosophy (B) fiction (C) ideal (D) inspiration
485. D	486. OFTEN is to SELDOM as BLACK is to (A) morning (B) darkness (C) white (D) dingy
538. B	539. BLASPHEME is to REVERE as COMPREHENSIBLE is to (A) composed (B) reprehensible (C) completed (D) inscrutable
591. B	592. INFANTRY is to FOOT as CAVALRY is to (A) horse (B) hoof (C) neigh (D) army
644. B	645. DOOR is to KNOB as HAMMER is to (A) handle (B) nail (C) wood (D) head

697. D	698. PISTOL is to TRIGGER as MOTOR is to (A) wire (B) dynamo (C) amperes (D) barrel (E) switch
750. D	751. RAISIN is to GRAPE as PRUNE is to (A) apricot (B) currant (C) plum (D) berry (E) peach
803. A	804. PROMISING is to PREGNANT as PREDATORY is to (A) raging (B) ravenous (C) adept (D) precious (E) dactile
856. B	857. CAT : FELINE :: (A) horse : equine (B) tiger: carnivorous (C) bird : vulpine (D) chair : furniture (E) sit : recline
909. A	910. CLASSIC : GREECE :: (A) Empire : France (B) Roman : Italy (C) colonialism : India (D) Ionic : Rome (E) new : America
962. D	963. ORGANISM : STIMULUS (A) horse : spur (B) bacteria : microscope (C) organ : dissection (D) frog : shock
1015. A	1016. RUSTICITY : URBANITY :: (A) silk : wool (B) rust : steel (C) caution : daring (D) publicity : television
1068. C	1069. CLOTHES : CLOSET :: (A) feet : rug (B) actor : script (C) ink : pen (D) beetle : insect
1121. A	1122. TADPOLE : FROG :: (A) gander : goose (B) caterpillar : butterfly (C) husband : wife (D) frog : fish
1174. B	1175. GALE : STORM (A) calorie : fat (B) shot : wound (C) robin : spring (D) table : legs
1227. A	1228. $2^2 : 3^3$ as 4 : (A) 4^4 (B) 27 (C) 5^5 (D) .4
1280. A	1281. PERSECUTE : PROSECUTE as HITLER : (A) jury (B) president (C) district attorney (D) sergeant at arms
1333. B	1334. OLFACTORY is to NOSE as TACTILE is to (A) tacit (B) bloody (C) finger (D) handkerchief (E) stomach

9. A	10. BED is to SLEEP as CHAIR is to (A) carry (B) sit (C) stare (D) awake
62. A	### 63. F. OBJECT TO ACTION RELATIONSHIP (Frames 64-81)
115. D	116. PEASANT is to HOVEL as KING is to (A) queen (B) royalty (C) crown (D) palace
	169. 2 is to 8 as 1/3 is to (A) 2/3 (B) 4/3 (C) 12 (D) 4
221. A	222. MIST is to SLEET as SIP is to (A) swallow (B) gulp (C) chew (D) devour
274. C	275. ARM is to LEG as FLIPPER is to (A) wing (B) tail (C) head (D) whale
327. A	328. RIVER is to STREAM as MOUNTAIN is to (A) cliff (B) hill (C) canyon (D) valley
380. C	381. BLADE is to GRASS as GRAIN is to (A) beach (B) sand (C) road (D) stone
433. A	434. ACT is to PLAY as CHAPTER is to (A) page (B) book (C) library (D) title
486. C	487. HOUSE is to MAN as TREE is to (A) woods (B) bird (C) family (D) spring
539. D	540. JEWELRY is to GOLD as COSMETICS is to (A) powder (B) face (C) eyes (D) woman
592. A	593. CAPT. is to CAPTAIN as LB. is to (A) building (B) oz. (C) pound (D) ton
645. A	646. BAY is to OCEAN as PENINSULA is to (A) continent (B) sea (C) gulf (D) island

698. E	699. CUBE is to PYRAMID as SQUARE is to (A) box (B) Egypt (C) pentagon (D) triangle (E) cylinder
751. C	752. CONSTELLATION is to STAR as ARCHIPELAGO is to (A) continent (B) peninsula (C) country (D) island (E) mono
804. B	805. OAT is to GRAIN as LARKSPUR is to (A) bird (B) mineral (C) horse (D) flower (E) animal
857. A	858. ADVERSITY : HAPPINESS :: (A) fear : misfortune (B) solace : adversity (C) vehemence : serenity (D) troublesome : petulance (E) graduation : felicitation
910. A	911. MARACAS : DANCER :: (A) xylophone : player (B) metronome : pianist (C) tambourine : gypsy (D) sample : salesman (E) wrench : plumber
963. A	964. FEATHERS : PLUCK :: (A) goose : duck (B) garment : weave (C) car : drive (D) wool : shear
1016. C	1017. MODESTY : ARROGANCE :: (A) debility : strength (B) cause : purpose (C) passion : emotion (D) finance : Wall Street
1069. C	1070. BLOW : HORN :: (A) cat : bowl (B) solve : problem (C) legislate : government (D) create : solution
1122. B	1123. UNITED STATES : NORTH AMERICA :: (A) Europe : France (B) New York : United States (C) England : Europe (D) North American : Europe
1175. C	1176. DECEMBER : WINTER (A) April : showers (B) August : summer (C) summer : June (D) March : spring
1228. B	1229. FLINT : (A) stone (B) fire (C) clap (D) flit as FLIRT : FLIGHT
1281. C	1282. REGENCY : EMPIRE as GOTHIC : (A) Romantic (B) Catholic (C) Byzantine (D) Remington
1334. C	1335. PARIAH is to OUTCAST as MULLAH is to (A) mourner (B) judge (C) martinet (D) constable (E) parish

10. B	11. DIESEL TRUCK is to OIL as PASSENGER CAR is to (A) gears (B) Chevrolet (C) gasoline (D) speed
	64. BOY is to TROUSERS as GIRL is to (A) overalls (B) suit (C) skirts (D) leather
116. D	117. FLOWERS is to VASE as MILK is to (A) udder (B) pitcher (C) farm (D) tube
169. B	170. 8 is to 2 as 4/3 is to (A) 8/3 (B) 1-1/3 (C) 1/3 (D) 8/6
222. B	223. TONE is to DEAFNESS as COLOR is to (A) seeing (B) blindness (C) focus (D) darkness
275. B	276. DOG is to CAT as SHEEP is to (A) wool (B) wolf (C) ewe (D) ram
328. B	329. SCULPTOR is to STATUE as PAINTER is to (A) brush (B) paint (C) artist (D) picture
381. B	382. SENATOR is to CONGRESS as LEAF is to (A) branch (B) root (B) bark (D) greenery
434. B	435. PRESIDENT is to CORPORATION as GOVERNOR is to (A) mayor (B) state (C) nation (D) government
487. B	488. BICYCLE is to MOTORCYCLE as WAGON is to (A) wheels (B) automobile (C) trailer (D) passenger
540. A	541. FAMINE is to FOOD as DROUGHT is to (A) river (B) irrigation (C) dam (D) water
593. C	594. THREE is to THIRD as ONE is to (A) fourth (B) third (C) second (D) first
646. A	647. MILK is to VOLUME as COAL is to (A) chimney (B) fuel (C) weight (D) heat

699. D	700. PROFIT is to SELLING as FAME is to (A) buying (B) cheating (C) bravery (D) praying (E) loving
752. D	753. ACCOUNTANCY is to BOOKKEEPING as COURT REPORTING is to (A) law (B) judgment (C) stenography (D) lawyer (E) judge
805. D	806. SPORT is to GOLF as GAME is to (A) cow (B) daring (C) chess (D) wolf (E) herd
858. C	859. NECKLACE : ADORNMENT :: (A) medal : decoration (B) bronze : medal (C) scarf : dress (D) window : house (E) pearl : diamond
911. B	912. LIQUOR : ALCOHOLISM :: (A) pill : dope (B) tranquilizer : emotions (C) perfume : smell (D) candy : overweight (E) atomizer : sinusitis
964. D	965. INTERRUPT : SPEAK :: (A) shout : yell (B) intrude : enter (C) interfere : assist (D) telephone : telegraph
1017. A	1018. ENCOURAGE : RESTRICT :: (A) gain : success (B) dearth : surplus (C) seeing : believing (D) heart : soul
1070. B	1071. SETTING : STONE :: (A) pen : holder (B) socket : bulb (C) picture : frame (D) pendulum : clock
1123. C	1124. ITALY : MILAN :: (A) Paris : Moscow (B) Moscow : Russia (C) Spain : Madrid (D) Manhattan : New York
1176. D	1177. CLOUDS : RAIN :: (A) wind : hurricane (B) thunder : lighting (C) water : H_2O (D) sky : universe
1229. D	1230. RADIUS : DIAMETER as (A) 3 (B) 4 (C) 5 (D) 6 : 8
1282. C	1283. (A) I (B) V (C) X (D) L : C as D : M
1335. B	1336. PLETHORIC is to SUPERFLUOUS as SUBLIMINAL is to (A) subterranean (B) subconscious (C) superb (D) fantastic (E) advertised

11. C	12. TASTE is to TONGUE as TOUCH is to (A) finger (B) eye (C) feeling (D) borrow
64. C	65. RASCAL is to LIE as GENTLEMAN is to (A) friend (B) reply (C) lady (D) truth
117. B	118. CRIMINAL is to PRISON as PATIENT is to (A) illness (B) doctor (C) cure (D) hospital
170. C	171. 144 is to 12 as 100 is to (A) 201 (B) 5,000 (C) 10 (D) 38
223. B	224. PRESIDENT is to NATION as MAYOR is to (A) ruler (B) state (C) city (D) governor
276. B	277. TABLE is to CLOTH as BED is to (A) blanket (B) mattress (C) pillow (D) spread
329. D	330. GOOD is to BETTER as WORST is to (A) terrible (B) worse (C) improvement (D) bad
382. A	383. BOYS is to MARBLES as GIRLS is to (A) women (B) jacks (C) school (D) delinquency
435. B	436. MONDAY is to FRIDAY as CHRISTMAS is to (A) Santa Claus (B) weekday (C) snow (D) Thanksgiving
488. B	489. SNOW is to WINTER as RAIN is to (A) wet (B) summer (C) cold (D) flood
541. D	542. LADDER is to RUNG as STAIRWAY is to (A) building (B) floor (C) step (D) escalator
594. D	595. PAST is to FUTURE as MEMORY is to (A) study (B) imagination (C) blank (D) brain
647. C	648. SONG is to TUNE as STATUE is to (A) cement (B) shape (C) melody (D) sculpture

700. C	701. BINDING is to BOOK as WELDING is to (A) box (B) tank (C) chair (D) wire (E) pencil
753. C	754. RUBBER is to FLEXIBILITY as PIPE is to (A) iron (B) copper (C) pliability (D) elasticity (E) rigidity
806. C	807. DISTANT is to REMOTE as NATIVE is to (A) indigenous (B) Indian (C) foreign (D) godly (E) ethical
859. A	860. GUN : HOLSTER :: (A) shoe : soldier (B) sword : warrior (C) ink : pen (D) books : school bag (E) cannon : plunder
912. D	913. MACE : MAJESTY :: (A) king : crown (B) sword : soldier (C) diploma : knowledge (D) book : knowledge (E) house : security
965. B	966. VIXEN : SCOLD (A) wound : scar (B) hero : win (C) bee : sting (D) pimple : irritate
1018. B	1019. DEBATE : SOLILOQUY :: (A) crowd : mob (B) Hamlet : Macbeth (C) Lincoln : Douglas (D) group : hermit
1071. C	1072. THREAT : INSECURITY :: (A) challenge : fight (B) reason : anger (C) thunder : lightning (D) speed : acceleration
1124. C	1125. LARGE : ENORMOUS :: (A) cat : tiger (B) warmth : frost (C) plump : fat (D) royal : regal
1177. A	1178. CRAWLING : FLYING :: (A) walking : swimming (B) triumph : victory (C) mortal : god like (D) bird : airplane
1230. B	1231. (A) reputable (B) canonical (C) referred (D) considered : AUTHORIZED as PROHIBITED : BANNED
1283. D	1284. CENTURY : (A) Middle Ages (B) Caslon (C) Finance (D) period as BODONI : GOUDY
1336. B	1337. SYSTOLE is to DIASTOLE as TRUNCATION is to (A) shortening (B) shrinkage (C) elongation (D) mutilation (E) trunk

12. A	13. LID is to BOX as CORK is to (A) preserver (B) bottle (C) whiskey (D) fire
65. D	66. BOYS is to CARPENTRY as GIRLS is to (A) knitting (B) dresses (C) pink (D) feminine
118. D	119. COUNTRY is to RAILROADS as BODY is to (A) arteries (B) hands (C) brain (D) muscles
171. C	172. 10% is to .2 as 30% is to (A) 50% (B) .5 (C) .6 (D) 100
224. C	225. BEG is to PLEAD as ALMS is to (A) beggar (B) selfishness (C) charity (D) philanthropist
277. D	278. SHOE is to FOOT as HAT is to (A) coat (B) hair (C) head (D) hat pin
330. B	331. STILLNESS is to NOISE as DARKNESS is to (A) daylight (B) moonlight (C) night (D) twilight
383. B	384. BIRDS is to SINGING as DOGS is to (A) chewing (B) barking (C) biting (D) stealing
436. D	437. TRAIN is to CONTINENT as STEAMSHIP is to (A) lane (B) ocean (C) planet (D) captain
489. B	490. HIM is to HE as ME is to (A) she (B) it (C) I (D) we
542. C	543. DISTANCE is to MEASUREMENT as MASS is to (A) pound (B) weight (C) matter (D) scale
595. B	596. DUPLICITY is to DISSIMULATION as GREED is to (A) creed (B) cupidity (C) need (D) grit
648. B	649. PEAK is to MOUNTAIN as COVE is to (A) canyon (B) plateau (C) ocean (D) lake

701. B	702. GYMNASIUM is to HEALTH as LIBRARY is to (A) sick (B) study (C) books (D) knowledge (E) school
754. E	755. ABSENCE is to PRESENCE as STABLE is to (A) steady (B) secure (C) safe (D) changeable (E) influential
807. A	808. BLAST is to GUST as BLARE is to (A) uncover (B) roar (C) blaze (D) icicle (E) trumpet
860. D	861. ARCHAEOLOGIST : ANTIQUITY :: (A) flower : horticulture (B) ichthyologist : marine life (C) theology : minister (D) Bible : psalms (E) gold : silver
913. C	914. COURT : JUSTICE :: (A) doctor : sickness (B) chief : boss (C) machinist : product (D) policeman : government (E) auditor : accuracy
966. C	967. SCHOOL : DISCIPLINE :: (A) pupil : dean (B) report card : marks (C) society : conformity (D) underworld : gangster
1019. D	1020. ATOM : ELECTRON :: (A) sun : earth (B) constellation : sun (C) sputnik : satellite (D) neutron : proton
1072. A	1073. FINGER : HAND :: (A) leg : toe (B) dictionary : word (C) toe : foot (D) medicine : doctor
1125. C	1126. COOLNESS : NIGHT :: (A) black : yellow (B) humidity : sunshine (C) warmth : day (D) fear : fright
1178. C	1179. GIRL : WOMAN :: (A) student : teacher (B) adult : child (C) black : white (D) infant : child
1231. B	1232. PEDAL : PIANO as (A) case (B) tune (C) rosin (D) bridge : VIOLIN
1284. B	1285. (A) literature (B) philosophy (C) art (D) music : PULITZER as PEACE : NOBEL
1337. C	1338. REGRESSIVE is to REGRESS as STERILE is to (A) sterilization (B) sterilize (C) sterility (D) sterilizer (E) storage

66. A	67. LETTERS is to MAILBOX as MONEY is to (A) coins (B) savings (C) bank (D) wealth
119. A	120. MONEY is to BANK as KNOWLEDGE is to (A) intelligence (B) blackboard (C) books (D) graduation
172. C	173. 1/16 is to 1/8 as 1/4 is to (A) 1/3 (B) 1/2 (C) 3/4 (D) 5/6
225. C	226. WATER is to CORK as AIR is to (A) sky (B) rubber (C) pressure (D) balloon
278. B	279. COMPOSER is to MUSIC as AUTHOR is to (A) typewriter (B) book (C) dramatist (D) character
331. A	332. INCLUDE is to OMIT as RECOGNIZE is to (A) notice (B) ignore (C) acknowledge (D) greet
384. B	385. IDIOT is to GENIUS as VALLEY is to (A) glen (B) mountain (C) water (D) alley
437. B	438. GOOD is to BETTER as MUCH is to (A) less (B) more (C) most (D) none
490. C	491. DREARY is to HAPPY as NARROW is to (A) light (B) wide (C) graceful (D) close
543. B	544. PLAY is to CURTAIN as SENTENCE is to (A) period (B) word (C) structure (D) grammar
596. B	597. BUILDING is to SEWING as CARPENTER is to (A) knitting (B) saw (C) seamstress (D) fence
649. D	650. ENCOURAGE is to INTIMIDATE as ALLOW is to (A) interdict (B) comply (C) expect (D) continue

702. D	703. COKE is to COAL as BREAD is to (A) eat (B) money (C) dough (D) man (E) yeast
755. D	756. SAFETY VALVE is to BOILER as FUSE is to (A) motor (B) house (C) wire (D) city (E) factory
808. B	809. DIURNAL is to DAILY as NOCTURNAL is to (A) evening (B) seasonal (C) equinocti (D) nightly (E) noxious
861. B	862. SHOE : LEATHER :: (A) passage : ship (B) trail : wagon (C) journey : boat (D) highway : asphalt (E) car : engine
914. E	915. PEDAGOGUE : LEARNING :: (A) teaching : books (B) professor : erudition (C) Plato : pedant (D) schoolmaster : ABC's (E) books : knowledge
967. C	968. THIRST : PARCH :: (A) fever : flush (B) water : sink (C) hunger : strangle (D) laughter : appease
1020. B	1021. STEP : STAIRWAY :: (A) staircase : banister (B) wood : carpet (C) rung : ladder (D) house : porch
1073. C	1074. FALL : PAIN :: (A) flying : walking (B) food : calories (C) disobedience : punishment (D) laugh : cry
1126. C	1127. CUT : HAIR :: (A) swim : pool (B) throw : ball (C) fall : step (D) tan : sun
1179. D	1180. FAMINE : HUNGER :: (A) conflagration : burning (B) pessimist : dismay (C) stupidity : failure (D) compound : mixture
1232. D	1233. PRODIGIOUS : (A) common (B) religious (C) capable (D) specious as CALLOUS : SOFT
1285. A	1286. (A) dock (B) boat (C) anchor (D) keel : PROW as KEY : RIBBON
1338. B	1339. MITOSIS is to DIVISION as OSMOSIS is to (A) diffusion (B) concentration (C) digestion (D) metamorphosis

15. PIG is to PORK
as STEER is to
(A) corral (B) ranch (C) beef (D) cowboy

67. C	68. ENEMY is to HATE as FRIEND is to (A) reject (B) contend (C) love (D) reply
120. C	121. SHIP is to DOCK as AUTOMOBILE is to (A) garage (B) compact (C) fender (D) mechanic
173. B	174. V is to L as C is to (A) I (B) D (C) M (D) LC
226. D	227. PIPE is to WATER as ARTERIES is to (A) veins (B) blood (C) boiler (D) heart
279. B	280. STEEL is to COMPOUND as IRON is to (A) compound (B) element (C) alloy (D) mixture
332. B	333. THUNDER is to NOISE as LIGHTNING is to (A) storm (B) flash (C) electricity (D) strike
385. B	386. LOVE is to CARESS as ANGER is to (A) emotion (B) glands (C) blow (D) murder
438. B	439. COUNTRY is to ARGENTINA as STATE is to (A) earth (B) Asia (C) Boston (D) Idaho
491. B	492. BRUNETTE is to BLOND as TRIVIAL is to (A) slight (B) foolish (C) unimportant (D) important
544. A	545. CANOE is to WOOD as BRIDGE is to (A) water (B) land (C) steel (D) transportation
597. C	598. STRONG is to IMPOTENT as POWERFUL is to (A) heroic (B) rocky (C) corrupt (D) ineffective
650. A	651. SPHERE is to CIRCLE as CUBE is to (A) ice (B) point (C) oval (D) square

703. C	704. INDIAN is to AMERICA as HINDU is to (A) Hindustan (B) Mexico (C) soil (D) magic (E) India.
756. A	757. SCHOLARLY is to UNSCHOLARLY as LEARNED is to (A) ignorant (B) wise (C) skilled (D) scholarly (E) literary
809. D	810. PEOPLE is to CROWD as SHEEP is to (A) goats (B) pasture (C) hills (D) mutton (E) flock
862. D	863. LORD : FEUDALISM :: (A) child : parent (B) farm : castle (C) entrepreneur : capitalism (D) laissez faire : tariff (E) conservative : radical
915. D	916. STICK : DISCIPLINE :: (A) bat : ball (B) carrot : incentive (C) hit : hurt (D) book : learning (E) seat : rest
968. A	969. MOSQUITOES : SCREEN :: (A) insects : annoyance (B) bugs : spray (C) wall : wind (D) sun : awning
1021. C	1022. FUTURE : HEREAFTER :: (A) recapitulation : repetition (B) past : present (C) idolatry : worship (D) prognosis : diagnosis
1074. C	1075. EYES : NOSE :: (A) arm : body (B) wood : desk (C) sidewalk : driveway (D) heel : sole
1127. B	1128. GIRL : WOMAN :: (A) dog : puppy (B) April : March (C) 8:00 P.M. : 7:00 P.M. (D) puppy : dog
1180. C	1181. 4 : 20 (A) 10 : 30 (B) 100 : 5 (C) 3 : 15 (D) 5 : 20
1233. A	1234. EACH OTHER : ONE ANOTHER as (A) marriage (B) dual (C) parrot (D) money : POLYGON
1286. D	1287. RHINESTONE : DIAMOND as (A) cloth (B) fruit (C) nylon (D) sheep : WOOL
1339. A	1340. FINIAL is to PINNACLE as PEDIMENT is to (A) basement (B) footing (C) gable (D) obstruction (E) pineal

15. C	16. FINDER is to REWARD as REPENTER is to (A) religion (B) sin (C) absolution (D) contrition
68. C	69. MISTAKE is to ERASER as CONSTITUTION is to (A) preamble (B) amendment (C) law (D) independence
121. A	122. SWIM is to POOL as BATHE is to (A) soap (B) tub (C) body (D) tile
174. C	175. **O. ASSOCIATION RELATIONSHIP** (Frames 176-181)
227. B	228. ATTACK is to PROTECT as OFFEND is to (A) combat (B) defend (C) conceal (D) reconciliate
280. C	281. ALLY is to ADVERSARY as WARM is to (A) equatorial (B) frigid (C) feverish (D) sunny
333. B	334. HEALTH is to SANITATION as DISEASE is to (A) filth (B) measles (C) carelessness (D) illness
386. C	387. IDEA is to WORDS as JUSTICE is to (A) blind (B) witness (C) law (D) iniquity
439. D	440. CARROT is to LETTUCE as POTATO is to (A) grape (B) cabbage (C) radish (D) onion
492. D	493. WINTER is to SPRING as DEATH is to (A) end (B) continuation (C) birth (D) sorrow
545. C	546. FISH is to SCALES as BIRD is to (A) nest (B) feathers (C) eggs (D) air
598. D	599. SKELETON is to BODY as FRAMEWORK is to (A) construction (B) house (C) mason (D) brick
651. D	652. CROWD is to PERSON as FOREST is to (A) ranger (B) fire (C) tree (D) grass

704. E	705. WEALTH is to MERCENARY as GOLD is to (A) Midas (B) miner (C) fame (D) eleemosynary (E) South Africa
757. A	758. IMMIGRANT is to ARRIVAL as EMIGRATION is to (A) leaving (B) alien (C) native (D) Italian (E) emigrant
810. E	811. PRESS is to PRINT as ERASER is to (A) efface (B) board (C) chalk (D) rubber (E) blot
863. C	864. FIN : FISH :: (A) engine : auto (B) propeller : aeroplane (C) five : ten (D) teeth : stomach (E) leg : chair
916. B	917. RESTRAIN : REPRESS (A) advance : capitulate (B) surround : surrender (C) march : refrain (D) retire : battle (E) urge : spur
969. D	970. CONCERT : MUSIC :: (A) performance : artist (B) exhibition : art (C) play : actor (D) operetta : singer
1022. A	1023. KEY : DOOR (A) combination : safe (B) keyhole : porthole (C) lock : key (D) opening : closing
1075. D	1076. THROW : BOUNCE :: (A) carry : lift (B) drop : break (C) catch : hop (D) hold : miss
1128. D	1129. AFTERNOON : DUSK :: (A) breakfast : dinner (B) yesterday : tomorrow (C) Sunday : Saturday (D) night : dawn
1181. C	1182. STUDYING : LEARNING :: (A) running : jumping (B) investigating : discovering (C) reading : writing (D) dancing : singing
1234. B	1235. READ : (A) scan (B) feel (C) dear (D) seen as SEAL : LEAS
1287. C	1288. GRAPE : PLUM as (A) tomato (B) banana (C) cabbage (D) coconut : PEACH
1340. C	1341. FLAMMABLE is to FIREPROOF as HALCYON is to (A) calm (B) heavenly (C) stormy (D) ancient (E) handy

16. C	17. SATISFACTION is to GOOD DEED as IMPROVEMENT is to (A) sin (B) fault (C) criticism (D) kindness
69. B	70. SEAL is to FISH as BIRD is to (A) wing (B) feather (C) worm (D) snail
122. B	123. BOOKS is to LIBRARY as WHEAT is to (A) oats (B) granary (C) breakfast (D) field
	176. PERFUME is to WOMAN as KIMONO is to (A) Japan (B) skirt (C) store (D) man
228. B	229. STEER is to RANCH as MEAT is to (A) carpenter (B) market (C) roast (D) cowboy
281. B	282. CELL is to TISSUE as TISSUE is to (A) system (B) organ (C) organism (D) mammal
334. A	335. STUDY is to LEARN as TRY is to (A) begin (B) attempt (C) fail (D) succeed
387. C	388. ALONE is to COMPANY as SAFE is to (A) solitude (B) assembly (C) danger (D) security
440. B	441. HOUR is to MINUTE as MINUTE is to (A) time (B) day (C) second (D) moment
493. C	494. WHEEL is to BUGGY as RUNNER is to (A) sled (B) horse (C) snow (D) race
546. B	547. CENTURY is to DECADE as DIME is to (A) lucre (B) cent (C) age (D) nickel
599. B	600. HONEY is to MILK as BEE is to (A) flower (B) farmer (C) pail (D) cow
652. C	653. MONTH is to MARCH as SEASON is to (A) May (B) snow (C) spring (D) flowers

705. A	706. BOTTLE is to BRITTLE as TIRE is to (A) elastic (B) scarce (C) rubber (D) spheroid (E) automobile
758. A	759. GOVERNOR is to STATE as GENERAL is to (A) lieutenant (B) navy (C) army (D) captain (E) admiral
811. A	812. ORANGE is to PEEL as PINE is to (A) needle (B) leaf (C) trunk (D) bark (E) woods
864. B	865. PULP : PAPER :: (A) rope : hemp (B) box : package (C) fabric : yarn (D) paper : package (E) cellulose : rayon
917. E	918. RUN : RACE :: (A) walk : pogo stick (B) swim : boat (C) fly : kite (D) sink : bottle (E) repair : automobile
970. B	971. OBSTRUCTION : BUOY :: (A) construction : building (B) boy : girl (C) danger : red light (D) iceberg : titanic
1023. A	1024. EXPEDITE : HASTEN :: (A) illuminate : disturb (B) refine : refute (C) inflate : distend (D) scour : squeeze
1076. B	1077. VIBRATION : SOUND :: (A) gravity : pull (B) watercolor : paint (C) accident : death (D) worm : reptile
1129. D	1130. WRITE : LETTER :: (A) pen : paper (B) drink : glass (C) act : part (D) memorize : book
1182. B	1183. DEPRESSION : MASOCHISM :: (A) man : animal (B) one : many (C) psychiatry : cure (D) revenge : sadism
1235. C	1236. $1-7/8 : 3-3/4$ as $3-1/4$: (A) $5-1/2$ (B) $2-3/16$ (C) $6-1/2$ (D) $1-1/4$
1288. A	1289. (A) ray (B) hose (C) socket (D) rain : DENIER as BULB : WATT
1341. C	1342. JABBER is to GIBBERISH as QUIDNUNC is to (A) quisling (B) gossip (C) theorist (D) testator (E) uncle

17. C	18. SEED is to PLANT as EGG is to (A) yolk (B) crack (C) bird (D) shell
70. C	71. POET is to POEM as AUTHOR is to (A) story (B) writer (C) content (D) rhyme
123. B	124. REVOLUTION is to LAND as MUTINY is to (A) captain (B) mutilate (C) bounty (D) sea
176. A	177. ROMANCE is to MOON as RIBBON is to (A) gift (B) horse (C) baloney (D) city
229. B	230. EASY is to HARD as SIMPLE is to (A) basic (B) simon (C) complex (D) fool
282. B	283. LAZINESS is to FAILURE as STRATEGY is to (A) mentality (B) brutality (C) company (D) victory
335. D	336. HEAL is to PHYSICIAN as LEND is to (A) money (B) banker (C) owe (D) give
388. C	389. NEAR is to NOWHERE as SOON is to (A) never (B) nearby (C) approximate (D) sporadic
441. C	442. PLATINUM is to TIN as DIAMOND is to (A) glass (B) ring (C) ruby (D) jewel
494. A	495. WOOD is to TABLE as TIN is to (A) metal (B) badge (C) pan (D) mine
547. B	548. SERVICE is to FEE as FAVOR is to (A) deed (B) request (C) person (D) thanks
600. D	601. FOUR is to THREE as SQUARE is to (A) rectangle (B) angle (C) triangle (D) box
653. C	654. LIKENESS is to PORTRAIT as TRUTH is to (A) falsehood (B) semblance (C) resemblance (D) event

706. A	707. PENINSULA is to MAINLAND as FIORD is to (A) boats (B) pay (C) sea (D) Massachusetts
759. C	760. LETTER CARRIER is to MAIL as MESSENGER is to (A) value (B) dispatches (C) easy (D) complicated (E) fast
812. D	813. ANT is to INSECT as FLUKE is to (A) error (B) chance (C) fish (D) hook (E) ensign
865. E	866. SKIN : MAN :: (A) scaled : fur (B) hide : hair (C) walls : room (D) roof : house (E) clothes : lady
918. C	919. ELIXIR : PILL :: (A) life : health (B) water : ice (C) bottle : box (D) mystery : medicine (E) nurse : doctor
971. C	972. FRUGAL : ECONOMICAL (A) fragile : solid (B) prosperous : wealthy (C) fruitful : sunny (D) regal : comical
1024. C	1025. MUNDANE : TEMPORAL :: (A) earthly : heavenly (B) celestial : starry (C) spiritual : everlasting (D) angelic : religious
1077. A	1078. CLARINET : MUSIC :: (A) symbol : sign (B) chalk : writing (C) daughter : father (D) pencil : pen
1130. C	1131. FURIOUS : ANGRY :: (A) cold : frozen (B) love : like (C) embrace : hug (D) slap : hit
1183. D	1184. MODERATE : EXTREME :: (A) cold : hot (B) tired : sleepy (C) liberal : radical (D) radical : reactionary
1236. C	1237. (A) will-o'-the-wisp (B) Ides of March (C) Scapa Flow (D) cat-o'-nine-tails : BROKEN MIRROR as THIRTEEN : THREE ON A MATCH
1289. B	1290. ARGONNE : (A) France (B) Oshkosh (C) Shiloh (D) Denver as LOCARNO : GENEVA
1342. B	1343. KEYNOTE is to TONIC as DIAPASON is to (A) gamut (B) clef (C) chord (D) organ (E) diaphragm

18. C	19. ASSIDUITY is to SUCCESS as CARE is to (A) avoidance (B) accident (C) fruition (D) safety
71. A	72. PSYCHIATRIST is to MALADJUSTMENT as DOCTOR is to (A) operation (B) disease (C) poverty (D) therapy
124. D	125. VINE is to MELON as TREE is to (A) limb (B) leaf (C) pear (D) earth
177. A	178. BULLET is to LEAD as MESSAGE is to (A) cartridge (B) barber (C) information (D) command
230. C	231. FLOUR is to WHEAT as GRAVEL is to (A) brick (B) rock (C) coal (D) bread
283. D	284. COLT is to STALLION as STREAM is to (A) water (B) river (C) brook (D) puddle
336. B	337. PERSON is to CROWD as TREE is to (A) wood (B) maple (C) forest (D) grass
389. A	390. ARMY is to ENEMY as UMBRELLA is to (A) ammunition (B) propaganda (C) weather (D) rain
442. A	443. FUR is to ANIMAL as WOOL is to (A) sheep (B) cloth (C) tiger (D) tailor
495. C	496. FOOT is to TOE as HAND is to (A) body (B) help (C) finger (D) manual
548. D	549. DISHONESTY is to INTEGRITY as OBVIOUS is to (A) oblong (B) invidious (C) surreptitious (D) honest
601. C	602. CITY is to PRETTY as COAT is to (A) beauty (B) boat (C) trousers (D) tailor
654. D	655. CREATE is to INVENT as DISCOVER is to (A) find (B) search (C) evolve (D) recover

707. C	708. HOUR is to MINUTE as MINUTE is to (A) man (B) week (C) second (D) short
760. B	761. CLOTH is to COAT as GINGHAM is to (A) doll (B) cover (C) washable (D) dress (E) dressmaker
813. C	814. JAIL is to CRIMINAL as ASYLUM is to (A) crazy (B) merman (C) psychic (D) degenerate (E) reprobate
866. D	867. RAIN : DROP :: (A) ice : winter (B) cloud : sky (C) flake : snow (D) ocean : stream (E) mankind : man
919. C	920. SCHOOL : LEARN :: (A) book : read (B) wheel : tire (C) knife : bread (D) press : print (E) teacher : learn
972. B	973. HORSE : CENTAUR (A) stable : barn (B) decade : century (C) pig : sty (D) fish : mermaid
1025. B	1026. MODEST : QUIET :: (A) cynical : determined (B) conceited : loquacious (C) capable : stubborn (D) egocentric : reserved
1078. B	1079. IMPORTANT : CRUCIAL :: (A) orange : lemon (B) sorrow : death (C) misdemeanor : felony (D) poverty : uncleanliness
1131. B	1132. WATER : SWIMMING :: (A) egg : frying (B) fire : flaming (C) chair : sitting (D) learning : knowledge
1184. C	1185. TOWER : CASTLE :: (A) car : motor (B) grass : prairie (C) house : chimney (D) rider : horse
1237. B	1238. (A) bullet (B) mortar (C) holster (D) trigger : GUN as MAN : BOY
1290. C	1291. GUSTATORY : TACTILE as (A) joint (B) flower (C) pickle (D) tongue : FINGER
1343. A	1344. POLTROON is to TERROR as PARANOIAC is to (A) courage (B) shyness (C) persecution (D) paralysis (E) responsibili

19. D	20. WINTER is to AUTUMN as SUMMER is to (A) month (B) spring (C) solstice (D) climate
72. B	73. CHECK is to FORGERY as COPYRIGHT is to (A) bank (B) infringement (C) book (D) author
125. C	126. SUBMARINE is to FISH as AIRPLANE is to (A) aquarium (B) bird (C) wing (D) hangar
178. C	179. RING is to WEDDING as CANNIBAL is to (A) rifle (B) savage (C) circle (D) kindness
231. B	232. SUDS is to DIRT as ERASER is to (A) gum (B) detergent (C) ink (D) pen
284. B	285. NEVER is to ALWAYS as SELDOM is to (A) frequently (B) sometimes (C) once in a while (D) occasionally
337. C	338. CARROT is to PLANT as COW is to (A) meat (B) herd (C) animal (D) stockyard
390. D	391. WELL-MANNERED is to COURTEOUS as GOOD is to (A) rustic (B) average (C) kind (D) in debt
443. A	444. COUNTERFEIT is to REAL as MATURE is to (A) spotted (B) rotten (C) unripe (D) grown
496. C	497. APRIL is to JUNE as JANUARY is to (A) month (B) March (C) February (D) beginning
549. C	550. FELT is to HAT as BRICKS is to (A) plaster (B) fire escape (C) bricklayer (D) building
602. B	603. HIGH is to RULER as HOT is to (A) weather (B) thermometer (C) climate (D) kettle
655. A	656. HONOR is to BRAVERY as GUILT is to (A) thief (B) crime (C) jail (D) killer

708. C	709. ABIDE is to DEPART as STAY is to (A) over (B) home (C) play (D) leave
761. D	762. BOAT is to **DOCK** as AIRPLANE is to (A) wing (B) strut (C) engine (D) wind (E) hangar
814. D	815. SUFFICIENT is to ENOUGH as SCARCE is to (A) fear (B) hardly (C) few (D) abundant (E) entire
867. E	868. RAISIN : PRUNE :: (A) apricot : currant (B) grape : plum (C) orange : grapefruit (D) kumquat : orange (E) citron : marmalade
920. D	921. PEOPLE : ELECT :: (A) statesman : govern (B) lawyer : debate (C) teach : teacher (D) diplomat : argue (E) journalist : news
973. D	974. JUSTICE : SCALES :: (A) ruler : education (B) weathervane : cock (C) tree : farm (D) court : crime
1026. B	1027. UXORIOUS : MISOGYNIST :: (A) philanthropic : charitable (B) useless : mystic (C) satanic : angelic (D) tender : gracious
1079. C	1080. RULE : KINGDOM :: (A) starvation : famine (B) discipline : children (C) proof : reason (D) reign : ruler
1132. C	1133. UNFRIENDLY : HOSTILE :: (A) weak : ill (B) weak : strong (C) blaze : flame (D) useful : necessary
1185. B	1186. PAMPHLET : BOOK :: (A) dress : sweater (B) discomfort : pain (C) height : weight (D) swimming : wading
1238. B	1239. MOVABLE : CAPABLE as KNOWLEDGEABLE : (A) credible (B) sensible (C) applicable (D) collegiate
1291. D	1292. VICTORY : PYRRHIC as FRUIT : (A) ripe (B) bitter (C) unexpected (D) tree
1344. C	1345. DISCIPLE is to MENTOR as PROSELYTE is to (A) opinion (B) expedition (C) leader (D) football (E) follower

20. B	21. WHEAT is to FLOUR as GRAPE is to (A) vintage (B) vine (C) wine (D) fruit
73. B	74. MAN is to OMNIVOROUS as LION is to (A) kingly (B) animal (C) carnivorous (D) omnipotent
126. B	127. HORSE is to STABLE as BABY is to (A) steep (B) young (C) house (D) cradle
179. B	180. 9 is to BASEBALL as 5 is to (A) basketball (B) odds (C) track (D) sports
232. C	233. DEBTOR is to CREDITOR as LIABILITY is to (A) marginal (B) depression (C) asset (D) profit
285. A	286. LOVE is to AMATEUR as WHITENESS is to (A) lonely (B) heart (C) candid (D) valentine
338. C	339. AIRPLANE is to PARACHUTE as BOAT is to (A) rescue (B) sink (C) life preserver (D) safety
391. C	392. PATTERN is to SHAPE as PLACE is to (A) corner (B) position (C) contour (D) symmetry
444. C	445. MOON is to EVENING as SUN is to (A) universe (B) rays (C) Phoebus (D) day
497. B	498. WEALTH is to POVERTY as SUCCESS is to (A) money (B) happiness (C) failure (D) future
550. D	551. FAINT is to LOUD as PINK is to (A) red (B) yellow (C) blue (D) white
603. B	604. SIXTEEN is to TWELVE as TWELVE is to (A) ten (B) nine (C) eight (D) seven
656. B	657. LACONIC is to DISTENDED as SUPPLE is to (A) tasty (B) limp (C) sloppy (D) given

709. D	710. JANUARY is to FEBRUARY as JUNE is to (A) July (B) May (C) month (D) year
762. E	763. OAT is to BUSHEL as DIAMOND is to (A) gram (B) hardness (C) usefulness (D) carat (E) ornament
815. C	816. TOOTH is to CHEW as STOMACH is to (A) develop (B) masticate (C) gastric (D) digest (E) assimilate
868. B	869. CONSTELLATION : STARS :: (A) state : country (B) library : book (C) archipelago : islands (D) continent : peninsula (E) dollar : penny
921. A	922. CALIBRATOR : MEASURE :: (A) plumber : wrench (B) clamp : hold (C) ruler : line (D) measure : tolerance (E) thermometer : temperature
974. B	975. PAPER : REAM :: (A) eggs : dozen (B) newspaper : stand (C) apartment : room (D) candy : wrapper
1027. C	1028. SAIL : SALE :: (A) cat : rat (B) blue : blew (C) tar : car (D) flew : flaw
1080. B	1081. SHAKESPEARE : IBSEN :: (A) Tolstoy : Keats (B) Aeschylus : Twain (C) Dickens : Milton (D) Joyce : Chaucer
1133. A	1134. EASTER : CHRISTMAS :: (A) opening : closing (B) holiday : school (C) end : beginning (D) New Year : Christmas
1186. B	1187. 90° ANGLE : RIGHT ANGLE: (A) talent : intelligence (B) crime : sickness (C) house : brownstone (D) temerity : boldness
1239. C	1240. PARANOIA : SCHIZOPHRENIA as (A) megalomania (B) carcinoma (C) hepatitis (D) glaucoma : MELANCHOLIA
1292. B	1293. SPAGHETTI : VODKA as (A) Florence (B) Henry (C) liquor (D) food : DON
1345. C	1346. SPLENETIC is to BENIGNANT as ENIGMATIC is to (A) turbid (B) pellucid (C) festoon (D) opacity (E) problematic

21. C	22. GRIEF is to WAR as HAPPINESS is to (A) joy (B) peace (C) soldier (D) finish
74. C	75. EGG is to BEAT as POTATO is to (A) hash (B) slash (C) eye (D) mash
127. D	128. TANK is to FISH as CAGE is to (A) bird (B) zoo (C) water (D) bars
180. A	181. CAGE is to BARS as BUILDING is to (A) water (B) bricks (C) food (D) country
233. C	234. WALK is to LIMP as TALK is to (A) pronunciation (B) stammer (C) crutch (D) speech
286. C	287. PAT is to TAP as TAR is to (A) rut (B) cur (C) pit (D) rat
339. C	340. TOASTMASTER is to BANQUET as CHAIRMAN is to (A) speaker (B) orator (C) assembly (D) speech
392. B	393. HAPPY is to SUCCESS as TIRED is to (A) relief (B) sleep (C) work (D) indolence
445. D	446. PRISON is to CRIMINAL as HOSPITAL is to (A) rich (B) ill (C) unforeseen (D) trained
498. C	499. TEACH is to SHOW as HATE is to (A) adore (B) injure (C) create (D) love
551. A	552. EVADE is to PURSUER as DODGE is to (A) ball (B) car (C) escape (D) blow
604. C	605. AXE is to HANDLE as WHEEL is to (A) car (B) full (C) garage (D) spoke
657. B	658. CLUB is to ADVISER as TEAM is to (A) mascot (B) player (C) member (D) coach

710. A	711. BOLD is to TIMID as ADVANCE is to (A) proceed (B) retreat (C) campaign (D) soldiers
763. D	764. PHYSIOLOGY is to SCIENCE as LAW is to (A) jurist (B) court (C) profession (D) contract (E) suit
816. D	817. DIN is to NOISE as CONTORTION is to (A) disease (B) writhing (C) exploitation (D) contingency (E) contour
869. C	870. BOOKKEEPER : ACCOUNTANT :: (A) reporter : editor (B) lawyer : judge (C) boy : man (D) typist : stenographer (E) teacher : student
922. B	923. AUTHOR : NOVEL:: (A) teacher : student (B) reader : interest (C) hero : conquest (D) carpenter : cabinet (E) doctor : cure
975. A	976. PLAY : SCRIPT :: (A) theatre : performers (B) peotry : anthology (C) script : handwriting (D) music : score
1028. B	1029 AMENITIES : GENTLEMAN :: (A) regulations : player (B) society : lady (C) profanity : hobo (D) requirements : professor
1081. B	1082. MEDICINE : SCIENCE :: (A) daughter : father (B) tomato : fruit (C) penicillin : aspirin (D) school : college
1134. C	1135. AIMLESSNESS : DELINQUENCY :: (A) aggression : appeasement (B) belligerence : mischief (C) slum : dirt (D) boredom : mischief
1187. D	1188. SADIST : INJURY :: (A) dentist : teeth (B) thief : robbery (C) priest : church (D) pupil : desk
1240. A	1241. GONDOLIERS : MIKADO as (A) Justice (B) Iolanthe (C) Macbeth (D) Faust : LOYALTIES
1293. A	1294. PRINCIPAL : (A) school (B) interest (C) idea (D) recess as RADIUM : WAVES
1346. B	1346. ANNULAR is to RING as NUMMULAR is to (A) limb (B) sum (C) shell (D) coin

22. B	23. MOON is to LIGHT as ECLIPSE is to (A) violence (B) darkness (C) cruelty (D) whistling
75. D	76. GUN is to SHOOT as CAR is to (A) enjoy (B) drive (C) move (D) repair
128. A	129. WATER is to AQUEDUCT as BLOOD is to (A) corpuscle (B) body (C) vein (D) plasma
181. B	182. **UNIT TWO: MISCELLANEOUS RELATIONSHIPS** ANALOGIES FOR GENERAL PRACTICE — STANDARD FORM MISCELLANEOUS RELATIONSHIPS (Frames 183-835)
234. B	235. CLAN is to FEUD as NATION is to (A) war (B) society (C) armaments (D) retaliation
287. D	288. DIVIDE is to MULTIPLY as SUBTRACT is to (A) plus (B) reduce (C) divide (D) add
340. C	341. MONTH is to WEEK as WEEK is to (A) day (B) month (C) year (D) hour
393. C	394. WIND is to CYCLONE as SHOWER is to (A) water (B) cloudburst (C) tornado (D) northeaster
446. B	447. BULL is to TOREADOR as DUCK is to (A) goose (B) hunter (C) rifle (D) barn
499. B	500. MAN is to BREAD as CATTLE is to (A) grass (B) milk (C) sheep (D) herd
552. D	553. SAVING is to POVERTY as VACCINATION is to (A) disease (B) doctor (C) needle (D) nurse
605. D	606. PENCIL is to LEAD as PEN is to (A) ink (B) story (C) blotter (D) school
658. D	659. ATHEIST is to AGNOSTIC as GODLESS is to (A) god-fearing (B) doubting (C) bigoted (D) pedantic

711. B	712. ABOVE is to BELOW as TOP is to (A) spin (B) bottom (C) surface (D) side
764. C	765. HUNGER is to INSTINCT as IMAGINATION is to (A) ideal (B) mind (C) thought (D) image (E) development
817. B	818. CONTINENCE is to RESTRAINT as CREVASSE is to (A) rift (B) glacier (C) depth (D) mountain (E) valley
870. A	871. RUBBER : FLEXIBILITY :: (A) iron : pliability (B) wood : plastic (C) steel : rigidity (D) iron : elasticity (E) synthetics : natural
923. D	924. CITIZEN : CONSTITUTION :: (A) alien : consul (B) emigrant : passport (C) resident : law (D) immigrant : visa (E) union : laborer
976. D	977. RECKLESSNESS : VALOR (A) courage : cowardice (B) reliance : dependability (C) restitution : confirmation (D) usury : interest
1029. A	1030. WICKED : SCORN :: (A) commendable : emulate (B) devilish : revere (C) celebrated : exculpate (D) weak : oust
1082. B	1083. BELL : RING:: (A) clock : build (B) alarm : sound (C) light : switch (D) scissors : handle
1135. D	1136. BOY : MAN :: (A) wall : floor (B) calf : cow (C) seat : chair (D) knob : door
1188. B	1189. PINK : RED :: (A) chartreuse : green (B) blue : turquoise (C) blue : pink (D) yellow : white
1241. A	1242. SALUTATORIAN : VALEDICTORIAN as (A) interruption (B) introduction (C) climax (D) repetition : CONCLUSION
1294. B	1295. BRAZIL : (A) nut (B) France (C) Spain (D) Portugal as CHILE : ECUADOR
1347. D	1348. DOWSER is to ROD as GEOMANCER is to (A) stones (B) maps (C) plants (D) configurations

23. B	24. HEAT is to FIRE as WATER is to (A) sky (B) rain (C) cloud (D) H_2O
76. B	77. ARTIST is to BRUSH as TAILOR is to (A) suit (B) stitch (C) needle (D) lapel
129. C	130. CAGE is to PARRAKEET as KENNEL is to (A) cat (B) animal (C) boxer (D) tunnel
	183. CONCLUSION is to ORIGIN as ANCIENT is to (A) bored (B) Greek (C) novel (D) marine
235. A	236. FAMINE is to ABUNDANCE as POVERTY is to (A) hunger (B) starvation (C) wealth (D) squalor
288. D	289. PORK is to PIG as MUTTON is to (A) wool (B) sheep (C) animal (D) farm
341. A	342. NIECE is to UNCLE as DAUGHTER is to (A) mother (B) aunt (C) father (D) grandfather
394. B	395. WATER is to THIRST as FOOD is to (A) supper (B) digestion (C) hunger (D) vegetable
447. B	448. THREAD is to TAILOR as SOLDER is to (A) lightning (B) rope (C) hod (D) welder
500. A	501. STUBBORN is to OBEDIENT as MULE is to (A) donkey (B) tail (C) horse (D) training
553. A	554. WATER is to RUBBER as FIRE is to (A) ashes (B) heat (C) asbestos (D) melting
606. A	607. FOOD is to COOKING as LETTERS is to (A) writing (B) paying (C) drawing (D) releasing
659. B	660. VICTORY is to CONTEST as KNOWLEDGE is to (A) professor (B) test (C) degree (D) study

712. B	713. LION is to ANIMAL as ROSE is to (A) smell (B) leaf (C) plant (D) thorn
765. B	766. CAPTAIN is to VESSEL as DIRECTOR is to (A) touring party (B) board (C) travel (D) orchestra (E) musician
818. A	819. COURTEOUS is to URBANE as EQUITABLE is to (A) equine (B) just (C) recurrent (D) ambiguous (E) equivocal
871. C	872. ABSENCE : PRESENCE :: (A) steady : secure (B) poor : influential (C) fresh : canned (D) safe : influential (E) stable : changeable
924. C	925. LAW : PROSECUTOR :: (A) constitution : Attorney general (B) Congress : President (C) legislation : governor (D) Bible : minister (E) athletics : boxer
977. D	978. RABBIT'S FOOT : FOUR-LEAF CLOVER :: (A) wishing well : pennies (B) devil : Satan (C) 13 : black cat (D) horseshoe : horse
1030. A	1031. SYMPATHY : ADVERSITY :: (A) acceptance : pathos (B) happiness : sadness (C) suppression : emotion (D) condolence : grief
1083. B	1084. FLUID : LIGHTER :: (A) wood : pencil (B) gas : automobile (C) chair : table (D) dust : chalk
1136. B	1137. BUTTON : SEAM :: (A) vest : suit (B) potato : eye (C) headlights : bumper (D) cake : fruit
1189. A	1190. FLY : FLOWN :: (A) see : saw (B) am : been (C) am : was (D) go : will go
1242. B	1243. FORTE : (A) mandolin (B) violin (C) piano (D) harp as HOI POLLOI : ARISTOCRACY
1295. D	1296. CERES : GRAIN as TERPSICHORE : (A) family (B) farmland (C) coffee (D) dance
1348. D	1349. ETYMOLOGY is to WORDS as HAGIOLOGY is to (A) saints (B) senility (C) selling (D) writing

24. B	25. NOISE is to DISTRACTING as HARMONY is to (A) harmful (B) loud (C) orchestrated (D) pleasing
77. C	78. PHYSICS is to MOTION as PHYSIOLOGY is to (A) function (B) geology (C) Newton (D) Pasteur
130. C	131. FRANC is to FRANCE as PESO is to (A) pizza (B) Mexico (C) pestle (D) England
183. C	184. THANKSGIVING is to NOVEMBER as CHRISTMAS is to (A) Santa Claus (B) December (C) snow (D) Jingle Bells
236. C	237. FUTURE is to PAST as UNKNOWN is to (A) past (B) indefinite (C) vague (D) known
289. B	290. MARE is to FILLY as KING is to (A) throne (B) prince (C) kingdom (D) majesty
342. C	343. BOOK is to PREFACE as HOTEL is to (A) room (B) guest (C) manager (D) lobby
395. C	396. SNOW is to SKI as ICE is to (A) sport (B) winter (C) swimming (D) skating
448. D	449. PLIERS is to MECHANIC as TROWEL is to (A) shovel (B) wheelbarrow (C) mason (D) cement
501. C	502. AUTOMOBILE is to TRAIN as CHAUFFEUR is to (A) engineer (B) driver (C) butler (D) servant
554. C	555. SATURNINE is to JOCOSE as OPULENCE is to (A) pollution (B) gem (C) opera (D) penury
607. A	608. EARS is to HEARING as NOSE is to (A) nostrils (B) perfume (C) glasses (D) smelling
660. D	661. LINE is to POINT as AREA is to (A) space (B) mathematics (C) line (D) ground

713. C	714. TIGER is to CARNIVOROUS as HORSE is to (A) cow (B) pony (C) buggy (D) herbivorous
766. D	767. OCEAN is to BAY as LAND is to (A) earth (B) home (C) peninsula (D) travel
819. B	820. CRYING is to TEARS as BREATHING is to (A) air (B) lungs (C) carbon-dioxide (D) nose (E) mouth
872. E	873. SAFETY VALVE : BOILER :: (A) fuse : motor (B) house : wire (C) city : factory (D) brake : automobile (E) extinguisher : fire
925. A	926. PORT : SHIP :: (A) ship : storm (B) home : sailor (C) garage : automobile (D) ground : plane (E) safety : danger
978. C	979. PLANE : AIR POCKET :: (A) vehicle : rut (B) hangar : airport (C) ground : sky (D) cabin : propeller
1031. D	1032. CRIMSON : RAGE :: (A) purple : purity (B) yellow : flag (C) red : danger (D) green : envy
1084. B	1085. PRISONER : JAIL :: (A) clock : time (B) ocean : beach (C) tiger : zoo (D) policeman : detective
1137. C	1138. PAINT : BRUSH :: (A) sing : music (B) play : work (C) cat : food (D) vault : pole
1190. B	1191. ARBITRATE : DISPUTE :: (A) solve : solution (B) regard : problem (C) settle : quarrel (D) organize : labor
1243. C	1244. CORNET : (A) oboe (B) drum (C) harpsichord (D) xylophone as GUITAR : CELLO
1296. D	1297. FRANKFURTER : (A) snack (B) hamburger (C) chicken (D) roll as SIRLOIN : PORTERHOUSE
1349. A	1350. EUPEPTIC is to DIGESTION as EUPHEMISTIC is to (A) speech (B) race (C) sound (D) drug

25. D	26. WOUND is to BLOOD as ACCIDENT is to (A) damage (B) case (C) car (D) murder
78. A	79. AMERICA is to COLUMBUS as TELEPHONE is to (A) ring (B) discovery (C) Bell (D) Edison
131. B	**132. J. DEGREE RELATIONSHIP** (Frames 133-144)
184. B	185. WEIGHT is to POUND as DISTANCE is to (A) inch (B) ruler (C) mileage (D) space
237. D	238. PRESSURE is to BAROMETER as FEVER is to (A) thermometer (B) speedometer (C) comptometer (D) perimeter
290. B	291. MOUSE is to CAT as SHEEP is to (A) wolf (B) skin (C) teeth (D) herd
343. D	344. RESOLVED is to DETERMINED as DESIRABLE is to (A) lovable (B) acceptable (C) pleasing (D) worthless
396. D	397. INFANT is to NURSERY as YOUTH is to (A) learning (B) school (C) adolescent (D) toys
449. C	450. PAYMENT is to DEBT as PREMIUM is to (A) cracker (B) prize (C) insurance (D) scarcity
502. A	503. FICTION is to NOVELIST as FACTS is to (A) legend (B) story (C) historian (D) research
555. D	556. TAP is to SHOVE as BREEZE is to (A) windmill (B) wind (C) coolness (D) tornado
608. D	609. SAM is to STAN as JOE is to (A) Henry (B) Abe (C) Jim (D) Marty
661. C	662. FOX is to CUNNING as SAGE is to (A) brains (B) student (C) school (D) wisdom

714. D	715. SAILOR is to NAVY as SOLDIER is to (A) gun (B) cap (C) hill (D) army
767. C	768. HATE is to LOVE as DESPAIR is to (A) grief (B) hope (C) failure (D) trouble
820. C	821. AX is to BLADE as SAW is to (A) sharp (B) teeth (C) ragged (D) metal (E) wood
873. A	874. SCHOLARLY : UNSCHOLARLY :: (A) learned : ignorant (B) wise : skilled (C) lies: knowledge (D) scholarly : literary (E) knowledge : books
926. C	927. BAY : PENINSULA :: (A) safety : danger (B) river : cape (C) mountain : hill (D) stand : sit (E) sea : land
979. A	980. BEHAVIOR : PSYCHOLOGIST :: (A) microbes : scientist (B) truth : philosopher (C) translation : linguist (D) prisons : criminologist
1032. D	1033. PLUTOCRACY : WEALTHY (A) autocracy : group (B) democracy : people (C) hierarchy : government (D) monarchy : tyrant
1085. C	1086. HANDCUFFS : ROBBER :: (A) leash : dog (B) rope : tie (C) shoes : feet (D) law : restriction
1138. D	1139. FRIDAY : TUESDAY (A) 3:00 AM : 11:00 AM (B) 6:00 PM : 10:00 AM (C) 7:00 PM : 11:00 PM (D) 5:00 AM : 9:00 PM
1191. C	1192. TELEPHONE : LETTER :: (A) loudspeaker : microphone (B) phonograph : manuscript (C) telegraph : telephone (D) sound : sight
1244. A	1245. RUTH : JEZEBEL as DAVID : (A) Matthew (B) Elisha (C) Luke (D) Peter
1297. B	1298. (A) coffee (B) milk (C) bottle (D) white : CREAM as SOUP : SALT
1350. A	1351. LOGGIA is to GALLERY as JALOUSIE is to (A) lintel (B) dowel (C) jamb (D) louver

26. A	27. HEAT is to RADIATOR as BREEZE is to (A) sea (B) ice cream (C) milk (D) fan
79. C	80. PERSON is to SKIN as NUT is to (A) peanut (B) elephant (C) salt (D) shell
	133. POSSIBLE is to PROBABLE as HOPE is to (A) expect (B) deceive (C) resent (D) prove
185. A	186. PAST is to REGRET as FUTURE is to (A) miss (B) hope (C) anticipate (D) foretell
238. A	239. SICKNESS is to HEALTH as DEATH is to (A) mortician (B) skull (C) life (D) pirate
291. A	292. TOMORROW is to YESTERDAY as FUTURE is to (A) present (B) unknown (C) year (D) past
344. B	345. IMPRISON is to JAIL as SPOUSE is to (A) ball and chain (B) wedding ring (C) wife (D) souse
397. B	398. LEAF is to TEA as BEAN is to (A) beverage (B) plant (C) coffee (D) hybrid
450. C	451. PROSE is to ESSAY as POETRY is to (A) sonnet (B) Virgil (C) verse (D) stanza
503. C	504. ELEPHANT is to MAN as TRUNK is to (A) trip (B) metal (C) body (D) hand
556. D	557. ENGINEER is to SEMAPHORE as PILOT is to (A) radio (B) airplane (C) stewardess (D) co-pilot
609. C	610. AMERICA is to AMERICAN as ITALY is to (A) countrified (B) Italian (C) national (D) European
662. D	663. LAND is to LAKE as SEA is to (A) fish (B) ocean (C) island (D) net

715. D	716. ODOR is to FLOWER as SOUND is to (A) noise (B) music (C) hear (D) bark
768. B	769. CARPENTER is to SAW as MASON is to (A) house (B) wall (C) man (D) trowel
821. B	822. COLD is to OVERCOAT as SUN is to (A) summer (B) earth (C) parasol (D) California (E) hot
874. A	875. IMMIGRATION : ENTRANCE :: (A) native : foreigner (B) emigration : departure (C) file : knife (D) travel : alien (E) nest : bird
927. E	928. HOTEL : SHELTER :: (A) bed : pillow (B) boat : transportation (C) train : ride (D) restaurant : drink (E) home : recuperation
980. B	981. URGE : INSIST :: (A) request : hound (B) plead : beg (C) refuse : deny (D) scourge : purge
1033. B	1034. ASCETIC : LUXURY :: (A) misogynist : women (B) philosopher : knowledge (C) capitalist : industry (D) general : victory
1086. A	1087. DISHONESTY : DISTRUST :: (A) violin : bow (B) hand : paper (C) money : thief (D) carelessness : accident
1139. C	1140. LUKEWARM : BOILING :: (A) cool : freezing (B) spending : buying (C) cold : hot (D) started : running
1192. D	1193. KITCHEN : CHEF :: (A) meat : refrigerator (B) restaurant : dining room (C) teamster : horse (D) office : typist
1245. B	1246. OBSTETRICIAN : OCULIST as (A) chiropodist (B) optometrist (C) chiropractor (D) gynecologist : PSYCHIATRIST
1298. A	1299. SILENTS : TALKIES as RADIO : (A) tube (B) broadcast (C) television (D) speaker
1351. D	1352. PHILIPPIC is to DEMOSTHENES as EUREKA is to (A) Aristotle (B) Phidias (C) Archimedes (D) Aristophanes

80. D	81. ENGINE is to FUEL as MAN is to (A) live (B) girl (C) work (D) food
133. A	134. GRAY is to BLACK as DISCOMFORT is to (A) green (B) pain (C) hospital (D) mutilation
186. B	187. RETARDATION is to DISPARAGEMENT as ACCELERATION is to (A) motor (B) encouragement (C) rapidity (D) calmness
239. C	240. INVENTOR is to MACHINE as AUTHOR is to (A) creator (B) poetry (C) book (D) computer
292. D	293. NONE is to LITTLE as NEVER is to (A) sometimes (B) frequently (C) negative (D) seldom
345. C	346. RECEPTION is to ADMISSION as SETTLE is to (A) resist (B) comfort (C) remain (D) adjust
398. C	399. DISHES is to BREAK as CLOTHES is to (A) wardrobe (B) tear (C) silverware (D) fall
451. A	452. NAVY is to ADMIRAL as CHURCH is to (A) bishop (B) Sunday (C) worshiper (D) sermon
504. D	505. ALIEN is to CITIZEN as FOREIGN is to (A) postal (B) ship (C) domestic (D) legion
557. A	558. STEP is to STAIRS as RUNG is to (A) rang (B) bell (C) ladder (D) ring
610. B	611. DAMP is to WET as GRAY is to (A) blue (B) hue (C) black (D) aged
663. C	664. TANGENT is to GEOMETRY as OBJECT is to (A) objection (B) name (C) boy (D) grammar

716. C	717. SUCCESS is to JOY as FAILURE is to (A) sadness (B) success (C) fail (D) work
769. D	770. DISLOYAL is to FAITHLESS as IMPERFECTION is to (A) contamination (B) depression (C) foible (D) decrepitude (E) praise
822. C	823. RUBBER is to ELASTIC as STEEL is to (A) metal (B) compound (C) girder (D) bridge (E) inflexible
875. B	876. GOVERNOR : STATE :: (A) lieutenant : army (B) inmate : institution (C) admiral : navy (D) ship : captain (E) mother : home
928. B	929. REWARD : PUNISHMENT :: (A) money : laughter (B) have : give (C) bravery : cowardice (D) medal : bravery (E) North : South
981. A	982. SWITCH : CURRENT :: (A) breeze : window (B) energy : resistance (C) tap : water (D) wind : sunshine
1034. A	1035. DINOSAUR : LIZARD :: (A) rattlesnake : python (B) mastodon : elephant (C) brontosaurus : pterodactyl (D) orang-utan : gorilla
1087. D	1088. ATOM : MOLECULE :: (A) vein : artery (B) branch : tree (C) capillary : heart (D) leg : toe
1140. A	1141. APPLE : PIE :: (A) potato : salad (B) yoke : egg (C) tank : fish (D) nest : bird
1193. D	1194. EIGHT : FOUR :: (A) fifty : twenty-five (B) forty : thirty (C) eighty : sixty (D) sixteen : sixty
1246. D	1247. HAIR : (A) epidermis (B) brain (C) shaggy (D) hat as SMOKE : CHIMNEY
1299. C	1300. ICE : STEAM as BRICK : (A) wine (B) honesty (C) pole (D) gas
1352. C	1353. PROLOGUE is to EPILOGUE as PROTASIS is to (A) epitome (B) epigenesis (C) apodosis (D) apogee

29. VERSAILLES is to PALACE
as BASTILLE is to
(A) parkway (B) Paris (C) prison (D) France

| 81. D | 82. G. SYNONYM RELATIONSHIP (Frames 83-97) |

| 134. B | 135. ORATION is to CHAT as BANQUET is to (A) festival (B) party (C) ball (D) snack |

| 187. B | 188. CONCEAL is to REVEAL as ASCEND is to (A) embark (B) descend (C) mount (D) leave |

| 240. C | 241. PICKLES is to JAR as GRAIN is to (A) fermentation (B) vintage (C) silo (D) satin |

| 293. D | 294. FOREST is to TREE as CROWD is to (A) alone (B) many (C) men (D) person |

| 346. D | 347. PLANS is to ARCHITECT as TREACHERY is to (A) thief (B) traitor (C) cheater (D) killer |

| 399. B | 400. CLIENT is to LAWYER as PATIENT is to (A) hospital (B) doctor (C) trial (D) illness |

| 452. A | 453. SOCIOLOGIST is to GROUP as PSYCHOLOGIST is to (A) delinquency (B) individual (C) brain (D) clinic |

| 505. C | 506. SPEAK is to SPOKE as TELL is to (A) sang (B) talk (C) told (D) singing |

| 558. C | 559. BIRD is to WINGS as FROG is to (A) legs (B) beak (C) pond (D) food |

| 611. C | 612. YEAR is to MONTH as MONTH is to (A) week (B) minute (C) time (D) hour |

| 664. D | 665. PIE is to CHERRY as SANDWICH is to (A) bread (B) mustard (C) ham (D) meal |

717. A	718. HOPE is to DESPAIR as HAPPINESS is to (A) frolic (B) fun (C) joy (D) sadness
770. C	771. NECKLACE is to PEARLS as CHAIN is to (A) metal (B) prisoner (C) locket (D) silver (E) links
823. E	824. OAK is to ACORN as VINE is to (A) shoot (B) grape (C) creeper (D) bower (E) wine
876. C	877. LETTER CARRIER : MAIL :: (A) messenger : value (B) message : messenger (C) government : fast (D) courier : dispatch (E) delivery : easy
929. C	930. VIBRATE : UNDULATE :: (A) sound : light (B) shudder : quiver (C) ripple : wave (D) flutter : waver (E) rattle : brandish
982. C	983. NEEDLES : SEWING :: (A) apples : sewing (B) scissors : cutting (C) sun : shine (D) airplane : traveling
1035. B	1036. BLOOD : ARTERY :: (A) water : pipe (B) anatomy : body (C) aorta : vein (D) thunder : lightning
1088. B	1089. LITMUS : ACID :: (A) metal : alloy (B) teacher : school (C) door : keyhole (D) telescope : object
1141. A	1142. WATER : ICE :: (A) lava : rock (B) soda : beer (C) snowflake : snow (D) iceberg : disaster
1194. A	1195. LOWER : RAISE :: (A) increase : augment (B) dissect : join (C) refuse : abandon (D) study : research
1247. A	1248. $12\text{-}1/2\% : 33\text{-}1/3\%$ as $14\text{-}2/7\% :$ (A) $9\text{-}1/5\%$ (B) $23\text{-}5/6\%$ (C) $16\text{-}2/3\%$ (D) $42\text{-}3/16\%$
1300. D	1301. FEVER : SPRING as (A) October (B) leaves (C) season (D) sadness : AUTUMN
1353. C	1354. SAUTEEING is to COOKERY as FAGOTING is to (A) juggling (B) forestry (C) embroidery (D) medicine

29. C	30. WINDOW is to PANE as DOOR is to (A) panel (B) knob (C) jamb (D) key
	83. GENEROUS is to PHILANTHROPIC as FRUGAL is to (A) parsimonious (B) benevolent (C) unhappy (D) wasteful
135. D	136. MOTORCYCLE is to BICYCLE as AUTOMOBILE is to (A) bus (B) airplane (C) transportation (D) wagon
188. B	189. ARTLESS is to SHREWD as SINCERE is to (A) sycophantic (B) sadistic (C) masochistic (D) critical
241. C	242. SKILLED is to MASTER as CLUMSY is to (A) gauche (B) amateur (C) infirmity (D) virtuoso
294. D	295. SCULPTOR is to STATUE as AUTHOR is to (A) writer (B) novel (C) manuscript (D) dictionary
347. B	348. HIDE is to LEATHER as FLINT is to (A) lighter (B) fuel (C) fire (D) heat
400. B	401. WOOD is to TABLE as STEEL is to (A) chair (B) iron (C) lumber (D) knife
453. B	454. MIMEOGRAPH is to INK as PAINT is to (A) paint (B) store (C) student (D) school
506. C	507. CORK is to LIGHT as LEAD is to (A) pencil (B) write (C) heavy (D) weight
559. A	560. COMPETITION is to MONOPOLY as IMMATURITY is to (A) anger (B) child (C) adult (D) incompatibility
612. A	613. KNEE is to LEG as ELBOW is to (A) wrist (B) arm (C) joint (D) bend
665. C	666. RUSSIA is to STEPPES as ARGENTINA is to (A) mountain (B) pampas (C) plateau (D) valley

718. D	719. PRETTY is to UGLY as ATTRACT is to (A) fine (B) repel (C) nice (D) draw
771. E	772. DRIFT is to SNOW as DUNE is to (A) hill (B) rain (C) sand (D) hail (E) desert
824. B	825. BIBLIOPHILE is to BOOKS as PHILATELIST is to (A) pharmacy (B) coins (C) stamps (D) jewelry (E) filament
877. D	878. WOOL : COAT :: (A) doll : cover (B) gingham : dress (C) cover : box (D) dressmaker : suit (E) yarn : wool
930. C	931. TRANSPARENT : TRANSLUCENT :: (A) water : milk (B) glass : water (C) translucent : opaque (D) clear : murky (E) angry : choleric
983. B	984. PAW : TAIL :: (A) cat : dog (B) toes : fingers (C) claw : cat (D) zipper : jacket
1036. A	1037. GELDING : STALLION :: (A) capon : rooster (B) chicken : duck (C) duck : drake (D) ram : ewe
1089. D	1090. DISCONTENT : STRIKE :: (A) friction : war (B) surgeon : operation (C) success : study (D) pay : job
1142. A	1143. CHURN : BUTTER :: (A) run : speed (B) milk : pail (C) distill : wine (D) defrost : meat
1195. B	1196. HIDE : SEEK :: (A) secrete : conceal (B) fur : animal (C) catch : toss (D) fly : swim
1248. C	1249. GOLD : YELLOW as (A) pink (B) white (C) black (D) blue : ROYAL
1301. B	1302. SUBMARINE : FISH as (A) kite (B) limousine (C) feather (D) chirp : BIRD
1354. C	1355. ACOLYTE is to ALTAR as CAMPANOLOGIST is to (A) tours (B) bells (C) scouts (D) politicos

30. A	31. COW is to GUERNSEY as DOG is to (A) canine (B) muzzle (C) collie (D) kennel
83. A	84. DOG is to CANINE as CAT is to (A) bovine (B) masculine (C) feline (D) tiger
136. D	137. SHOWER is to CLOUDBURST as BREEZE is to (A) rain (B) sunshine (C) climate (D) cyclone
189. A	190. ANARCHY is to DEMOCRACY as DISCORD is to (A) difference (B) confusion (C) disagreement (D) adaptation
242. B	243. TEMPERATURE is to THERMOMETER as TIME is to (A) minutes (B) day (C) clock (D) flies
295. B	296. WHOLE is to PART as CANADA is to (A) United State (B) Ottawa (C) Ontario (D) North America
348. C	349. RECURRENCE is to PERIODIC as DETERMINATION is to (A) cowardly (B) persevering (C) hopeless (D) literary
401. D	402. LAW BREAKER is to BAIL as HOSTAGE is to (A) criminal (B) ransom (C) murder (D) threat
454. A	455. CEILING is to CHANDELIER as PUPPETEER is to (A) puppet show (B) puppet maker (C) puppet (D) pup
507. C	508. DIME is to SILVER as BULLET is to (A) gun (B) bandit (C) lead (D) copper
560. C	561. SLAP is to DISAPPROVE as REPROVE is to (A) denounce (B) disprove (C) flatter (D) improve
613. B	614. CHARITY is to SELFISHNESS as ANGEL is to (A) cake (B) harp (C) devil (D) heaven
666. B	667. POCKET is to PANTS as PIGEONHOLE is to (A) desk (B) wing (C) bird (D) sparrow

719. B	720. PUPIL is to TEACHER as CHILD is to (A) parent (B) dolly (C) youngster (D) obey
772. C	773. DILIGENT is to UNREMITTING as DIAMETRIC is to (A) pretentious (B) geographical (C) adamant (D) contrary (E) opposite
825. C	826. NYMPH is to WATER as DRYAD is to (A) land (B) tree (C) elm (D) wringer (E) advertisement
878. B	879. BOAT : DOCK :: (A) wing : strut (B) engine : chassis (C) contents : box (D) verb : sentence (E) dirigible : hangar
931. C	932. HEROISM : REWARD :: (A) wish : dried (B) civilian : criminal (C) misdemeanor : felony (D) trespassing : burglary (E) crime : punishment
984. B	985. GEAR : MACHINE :: (A) shoe : walking (B) coat : label (C) sail : boat (D) eraser : paper
1037. A	1038. BOOK : LIBRARY :: (A) dish : closet (B) towel : laundry (C) student : professor (D) page : print
1090. A	1091. BRAKE : WHEEL (A) ban : action (B) car : tire (C) charity : wealth (D) stop : start
1143. C	1144. FISH : SWIM :: (A) snake : bite (B) ant : crawl (C) buffalo : roar (D) frog : breathe
1196. C	1197. SMOKE : FIRE :: (A) flame : charcoal (B) cooperation : goodness (C) burn : wound (D) water : smoke
1249. D	1250. (A) rants (B) dance (C) ants (D) pain : PANTS as INCH : PINCH
1302. A	1303. (A) horse (B) dog (C) duck (D) tiger : LADY as CAT : WOLF
1355. B	1356. BRASS is to COPPER as PEWTER is to (A) lead (B) zinc (C) silver (D) bronze

31. C	32. PLAY is to PROLOGUE as CONSTITUTION is to (A) preamble (B) laws (C) Washington (D) country
84. C	85. PLEASURE is to ENJOYMENT as HATE is to (A) Satan (B) love (C) fate (D) abhorrence
137. D	138. SIN is to EVIL as TOOTHPICK is to (A) tooth (B) log (C) food (D) dentist
190. D	191. CAPE is to CONTINENT as GULF is to (A) ocean (B) lake (C) reservoir (D) water
243. C	244. FEVER is to SICKNESS as CLOUD is to (A) sky (B) cold (C) storm (D) weather
296. C	297. BRAY is to DONKEY as BARK is to (A) tree (B) dog (C) covering (D) park
349. B	350. CHEMISTRY is to ELEMENTS as GRAMMAR is to (A) teacher (B) English (C) subject (D) parts of speech
402. B	403. FOOD is to BACTERIA as VALID CONCLUSION is to (A) going to school (B) environment (C) loose thinking (D) parental influence
455. C	456. MILK is to CONTAINER as JELLY is to (A) raspberry (B) sugar (C) apple (D) jar
508. C	509. PUGNACIOUS is to FIGHT as DISHONEST is to (A) win (B) help (C) pity (D) cheat
561. A	562. KNIFE is to GRIND as STOCKING is to (A) wear (B) tear (C) see (D) darn
614. C	615. EAT is to BREAD as WEAR is to (A) store (B) coat (C) wool (D) sheep
667. A	668. DEPENDENT is to AUTONOMY as SUBSERVIENT is to (A) servant (B) submarine (C) monarch (D) offering

720. A	721. CITY is to MAYOR as ARMY is to (A) navy (B) soldier (C) general (D) private
773. E	774. GALLEY is to VESSEL as PERSIMMON is to (A) machine (B) fruit (C) engine (D) vehicle (E) communication
826. B	827. HEART is to BODY as ENGINE is to (A) mind (B) machine (C) combustion (D) electricity (E) engineer
879. E	880. OAT : BUSHEL :: (A) wheat : gram (B) hardness : usefulness (C) gold : karat (D) diamond : carat (E) ornament : case
932. E	933. REFORM : RECIDIVISM :: (A) crime : prison (B) dilettante : professional (C) divorce : alimony (D) connoisseur : judge (E) probation : parole
985. C	986. BLOW : HORN :: (A) eat : dish (B) legislate : government (C) create : picture (D) solve : problem
1038. A	1039. OBSOLETE : CURRENT :: (A) candle : electricity (B) buggy : automobile (C) certainty : doubt (D) blackberry : jelly
1091. A	1092. SLICE : BREAD :: (A) submarine : water (B) termite : wood (C) leaf : tree (D) fish : water
1144. B	1145. AUGUST : JULY :: (A) 5 : 4 (B) year : month (C) 10 : 11 (D) month : day
1197. B	1198. TRIANGLE : HEXAGON :: (A) rectangle : circle (B) quadrilateral : trapezoid (C) square : octagon (D) polygon : parallelogram
1250. C	1251. HALF-MAST : ELEGY as (A) return (B) speech (C) dawn (D) plot : INCEPTION
1303. C	1304. STALAGMITE : STALACTITE as FLOOR : (A) chemical (B) tally (C) rock (D) roof
1356. A	1357. CAPE is to PROMONTORY as WADI is to (A) river (B) waterfall (C) meadow (D) fen

32. A	33. ENGLAND is to LONDON as CANADA is to (A) Montreal (B) Ontario (C) Quebec (D) Banff
85. D	86. BOSS is to FOREMAN as PRESIDENT is to (A) manager (B) employee (C) nation (D) congress
138. B	139. INFANT is to ADULT as KITTEN is to (A) dog (B) cat (C) pig (D) giraffe
191. A	192. KNOT is to WATER as MILE is to (A) boat (B) inch (C) land (D) rod
244. C	245. SWEET is to SUGAR as BITTER is to (A) malaria (B) quinine (C) saccharine (D) acidity
297. B	298. PICTURE is to ARTIST as BOOK is to (A) page (B) print (C) author (D) read
350. D	351. LIBRARIAN is to LIBRARY as TEACHER is to (A) school (B) principal (C) classroom (D) education
403. C	404. KENNEL is to FUNNEL as HOUSE is to (A) wood (B) chase (C) dog (D) cat
456. D	457. HORSE is to HOOF as MAN is to (A) shoe (B) foot (C) walk (D) lace
509. D	510. ILLINOIS is to CHICAGO as MASSACHUSETTS is to (A) Boston (B) Kentucky (C) New York (D) Europe
562. D	563. SCISSORS is to CLOTH as SAW is to (A) teeth (B) knife (C) board (D) blade
615. B	616. FRIDAY is to SATURDAY as MONDAY is to (A) week (B) Sunday (C) month (D) Tuesday
668. C	669. POSTPONEMENT is to BEGINNING as LATENESS is to (A) haste (B) tardiness (C) school (D) carelessness

721. **C**	**722.** ESTABLISH is to BEGIN as ABOLISH is to (A) slavery (B) wrong (C) abolition (D) end
774. **B**	**775.** BANDAGE is to WOUND as STRING is to (A) package (B) sling (C) rope (D) twine
827. **B**	**828.** AIRPLANE is to TRANSPORTATION as WIRELESS is to (A) message (B) speed (C) trans-oceanic (D) communication (E) radio
880. **D**	**881.** PHYSIOLOGY : SCIENCE :: (A) psychology : psychiatry (B) profession : law (C) contract: suit (D) painting: art (E) worker: work
933. **B**	**934.** DISCRIMINATE : SEGREGATE :: (A) select : separate (B) good : best (C) sift : unravel (D) blend : fuse (E) convict : punish
986. **D**	**987.** LEG : WALKING :: (A) harp : stringing (B) brain : thinking (C) body : playing (D) lion : roaring
1039. **B**	**1040.** BOREDOM : VARIETY :: (A) fun : Coney Island (B) tears : regrets (C) play : work (D) sadness : jest
1092. **C**	**1093.** RADIATOR : HEAT :: (A) growth : plant (B) lamp : light (C) water : sun (D) branch : tree
1145. **A**	**1146.** IRON : RIGID :: (A) ice-cream : firm (B) ball : circular (C) rubber : flexible (D) hand : finger
1198. **C**	**1199.** CENTURY : MILLENIUM :: (A) decade : century (B) epoch : era (C) age : epic (D) month : year
1251. **C**	**1252.** HERD : (A) page (B) sin (C) cattle (D) flock as SALT : ICON
1304. **D**	**1305.** HARVARD : YALE as SMITH : (A) Princeton (B) Purdue (C) Columbia (D) Dartmouth
1357. **A**	**1358.** CATALYST is to CHANGE as ACCELERATOR is to (A) cylinder (B) inertia (C) motion (D) exhaust

33. A	34. PARAGRAPH is to SENTENCE as SENTENCE is to (A) clause (B) word (C) composition (D) correctness
86. A	87. DIG is to EXCAVATE as KILL is to (A) try (B) avenge (C) convict (D) slay
139. B	140. HUMMINGBIRD is to EAGLE as SHRUB is to (A) forest (B) mountain (C) grass (D) tree
192. C	193. AGGRAVATE is to EASE as ENERVATE is to (A) end (B) invigorate (C) retire (D) unnerve
245. B	246. STONE is to QUARRY as LUMBER is to (A) crystallization (B) mine (C) foliage (D) forest
298. C	299. PICTURE is to SEE as SPEECH is to (A) view (B) hear (C) enunciate (D) soliloquize
351. C	352. SMALLNESS is to MAGNITUDE as PRESENT is to (A) attendance (B) existing (C) absent (D) tense
404. B	405. STAR is to FLAG as EAR is to (A) face (B) head (C) cheek (D) hearing
457. B	458. IDIOT is to GENIUS as VALLEY is to (A) plateau (B) moron (C) mountain (D) field
510. A	511. LOSE is to HAVE as GO is to (A) remove (B) invite (C) stay (D) evacuate
563. C	564. STRENGTH is to POWER as LUCK is to (A) horseshoe (B) faith (C) Halloween (D) happiness
616. D	617. ROSE is to PLANT as LION is to (A) animal (B) fur (C) king (D) paw
669. A	670. SOPRANO is to HIGH as BASS is to (A) violin (B) good (C) low (D) fish (E) soft.

722. D	723. DECEMBER is to JANUARY as LAST is to (A) least (B) worst (C) month (D) first
775. A	776. LIQUID is to SIPHON as SMOKE is to (A) chimney (B) fire (C) flame (D) flue (E) tobacco
828. D	829. AGRICULTURE is to FARMER as INDUSTRY is to (A) retailer (B) manufacturer (C) wholesaler (D) financier (E) entrepreneur
881. D	882. INSTINCT : LEARNING :: (A) reflex : will (B) thought : idea (C) sight : image (D) development : project (E) research : development
934. A	935. EMULATE : MIMIC :: (A) slander : defame (B) praise : flatter (C) express : imply (D) complain : condemn (E) act : declaim
987. B	988. PUPIL : CORNEA :: (A) teacher : pupil (B) page : print (C) peg : board (D) success : money
1040. D	1041. SQUARE : DIAMOND :: (A) cube : sugar (B) circle : ellipse (C) innocence : jewelry (D) rectangle : square
1093. B	1094. WOODSMAN : AX :: (A) mechanic : tool (B) carpenter : saw (C) draftsman : ruler (D) doctor : prescription
1146. C	1147. BIGOTRY : HATRED (A) sweetness : bitterness (B) segregation : integration (C) equality : government (D) fanaticism : intolerance
1199. A	1200. PROPRIETOR : MANAGER (A) employee : secretary (B) foreman : supervisor (C) laborer : capitalist (D) superintendent : attendant
1252. A	1253. NEWTON : COPERNICUS as SHAKESPEARE : (A) Jackson (B) Jonson (C) Dickens (D) Pope
1305. D	1306. CHEVROLET : CADILLAC as BEAVER : (A) Chrysler (B) mink (C) chauffeur (D) Boeing
1358. C	1359. CATAMARAN is to RAFT as TERMAGANT is to (A) grisette (B) benedict (C) spinster (D) shrew

34. B	35. NUT is to SHELL as PEA is to (A) shooter (B) soup (C) green (D) pod
87. D	88. PERSISTENT is to OBSTINACY as VALIANT is to (A) value (B) warfare (C) village (D) bravery
140. D	141. FLEA is to HORSEFLY as MINNOW is to (A) eagle (B) whale (C) giant (D) elephant
193. B	194. VISION is to LENS as WALKING is to (A) legs (B) paralysis (C) doctor (D) crutch
246. D	247. LEGAL is to TRIAL as LAWLESS is to (A) witness (B) oath (C) lynching (D) martial
299. B	300. TORNADO is to BREEZE as SHOVE is to (A) shovel (B) stove (C) tap (D) rap
352. C	353. DELUSION is to ILLUSION as INVALIDATE is to (A) vote (B) approve (C) advocate (D) abrogate
405. B	406. WHOLE is to PART as UNITED STATES is to (A) universe (B) land (C) sea (D) Illinois
458. C	459. LIES is to LAIN as DRINKS is to (A) drunk (B) drink (C) drinked (D) drank
511. C	512. PLETHORA is to DEARTH as CUNNING is to (A) dull (B) earthy (C) foxy (D) cute
564. A	564. TRACTOR is to HANDPLOW as ELEVATOR is to (A) building (B) skyscraper (C) stairs (D) feet
617. A	618. OAK is to WOOD as MARBLE is to (A) stone (B) table (C) house (D) tree
670. C	671. STREET is to HORIZONTAL as BUILDING is to (A) tall (B) brick (C) broad (D) vertical (E) large

723. D	724. GIANT is to DWARF as LARGE is to (A) big (B) monster (C) queer (D) small
776. D	777. EXTORT is to WREST as CONSPIRE is to (A) entice (B) plot (C) deduce (D) respire (E) convey
829. B	830. HORSE is to HITCHING-POST as CRAFT is to (A) parapet (B) moorage (C) cunning (D) vessel (E) cheese
882. A	883. CAPTAIN : VESSEL :: (A) guide : touring party (B) boat : travel (C) conductor : train (D) conductor : orchestra (E) musician : violin
935. B	936. ASSIST : SAVE :: (A) agree : oppose (B) rely : descry (C) request : command (D) declare : deny (E) help : aid
988. A	989. 2 : 5 :: (A) 5 : 7 (B) 6 : 17 (C) 6 : 15 (D) 5 : 14
1041. B	1042. DOUBLEHEADER : TRIDENT :: (A) twin : troika (B) ballgame : three bagger (C) chewing gum : toothpaste (D) freak : zoo
1094. B	1095. BOUQUET : FLOWER (A) key : door (B) air : balloon (C) skin : body (D) chain : link
1147. D	1148. LETTER : WORD :: (A) club : people (B) homework : school (C) page : book (D) product : factory
1200. B	1201. SQUARE YARD : SQUARE FOOT :: (A) foot : inch (B) square : cube (C) 9 : 1 (D) man : boy
1253. B	1254. SLEDS : RUNNERS as (A) trains (B) wounds (C) athletes (D) skates : BLADES
1306. B	1307. TABARD : CHAUCER as (A) Admiral Benbow (B) Major Andre (C) Sergeant York (D) General Pershing : STEVENSON
1359. D	1360. CINCTURE is to WAIST as SPHINCTER is to (A) didoes (B) bone splint (C) blood clot (D) orifice

35. D	36. ANTLER is to DEER as TUSK is to (A) husk (B) tooth (C) elephant (D) animal
88. D	89. SMALL is to DWARF as LARGE is to (A) shark (B) fish (C) animal (D) giant
141. B	142. PROBABLE is to CERTAIN as APPROACH is to (A) nearness (B) reproach (C) possibility (D) destination
194. D	195. BUS is to ROAD as LOCOMOTIVE is to (A) wheels (B) steel (C) steam (D) rails
247. C	248. YEAR is to JULY as WEEK is to (A) Wednesday (B) fortnight (C) month (D) century
300. C	301. JOHN HANCOCK is to DECLARATION OF INDEPENDENCE as GEORGE WASHINGTON is to (A) cherry tree (B) Valley Forge (C) Mt. Vernon (D) Martha Washington
353. D	354. NORMAL is to NEUROTIC as harmless is to (A) helpful (B) harmful (C) unharmed (D) dog
406. D	407. WINE is to DREGS as WHEAT is to (A) bushel (B) chaff (C) stalk (D) bread
459. A	460. BOTANIST is to PLANTS as GEOLOGIST is to (A) trees (B) structure (C) geography (D) quartz
512. A	513. DOG is to KENNEL as KING is to (A) palace (B) house (C) queen (D) royalty
565. C	566. MACHINIST is to METAL as MASON is to (A) horse (B) wood (C) mechanics (D) stone
618. A	619. WOLF is to DOG as TIGER is to (A) cat (B) stripes (C) snap (D) paw
671. D	672. PREDICAMENT is to CARELESSNESS as RESPONSE is to (A) answer (B) stimulus (C) correct (D) effect (E) good

724. D	725. ENGINE is to CABOOSE as BEGINNING is to (A) commence (B) cabin (C) end (D) train
777. B	778. WIDOW is to DOWAGER as CONSORT is to (A) enemy (B) constable (C) companion (D) distaff (E) curette
830. B	831. BALL is to BAT as SHUTTLE-COCK is to (A) battledore (B) badminton (C) turkey (D) game (E) plumage
883. D	884. FATHER : DAUGHTER :: (A) son : daughter (B) uncle : nephew (C) uncle : aunt (D) son-in-law : daughter (E) grandfather : mother
936. C	937. INFATUATION : LOVE :: (A) youth : fancy (B) obsession : interest (C) June : wedding (D) cupid : arrow
989. C	990. STOVE : KITCHEN :: (A) window : bedroom (B) sink : bathroom (C) television : livingroom (D) trunk : attic
1042. A	1043. CELEBRATE : MARRIAGE :: (A) announce : birthday (B) report : injury (C) lament : bereavement (D) face : penalty
1095. D	1096. BUTTON : ZIPPER :: (A) thread : needle (B) cloth : material (C) margarine : butter (D) vitamin : health
1148. C	1149. NEGLIGENT : REQUIREMENT :: (A) careful : position (B) remiss : duty (C) cautious : injury (D) cogent : task
1201. C	1202. LOUD : THUNDER :: (A) simple : person (B) flashy : lightning (C) ferocious : tiger (D) meat : sweet
1254. D	1255. CONN. : WASH. as (A) Iowa (B) Miss. (C) Ohio (D) Idaho : ARIZ.
1307. A	1308. (A) Pluto (B) Arthur (C) nut (D) acronym : SURNAME as WAC : JONES
1360. D	1361. DEBIT is to CREDIT as DENOUEMENT is to (A) climax (B) outcome (C) complication (D) untying

36. C	37. NECKLACE is to BEAD as CHAIN is to (A) ball (B) iron (C) link (D) strength
89. D	90. COINS is to NUMISMATIST as STAMPS is to (A) scientist (B) philatelist (C) anarchist (D) machinist
142. D	143. AUTOMOBILE is to HORSE as TELEGRAM is to (A) telephone (B) letter (C) communication (D) transportation
195. D	196. MOUNTAIN is to PEAK as WAVE is to (A) water (B) storm (C) crest (D) ocean
248. A	249. FOOD is to BODY as FUEL is to (A) engine (B) kite (C) ball (D) mechanic
301. B	302. LOOK is to SEE as LISTEN is to (A) illuminate (B) audition (C) hear (D) hearken
354. B	355. EMENDATION is to ERRONEOUS as CLARIFICATION is to (A) nebulous (B) correction (C) criticism (D) failure
407. B	408. LABYRINTH is to MAZE as ENIGMA is to (A) puzzle (B) string (C) alternative (D) sphinx
460. B	461. TEMPORARY is to PERMANENT as EPHEMERAL is to (A) elongated (B) useless (C) everlasting (D) heavenly
513. A	514. OFFICE is to TYPIST as FACTORY is to (A) mechanic (B) machinery (C) smoke (D) production
566. D	567. NOVICE is to INSECURITY as EXPERT is to (A) tools (B) confidence (C) difficulty (D) money
619. A	620. SADNESS is to FAILURE as JOY is to (A) work (B) job (C) luck (D) success
672. B	673. CANVAS is to PAINT as CLAY is to (A) mold (B) cloth (C) statue (D) art (E) aesthetic

725. C	726. DISMAL is to CHEERFUL as DARK is to (A) sad (B) stars (C) night (D) bright
778. C	779. EMINENT is to LOWLY as FREQUENT is to (A) often (B) frivolous (C) enhance (D) soon (E) rare
831. A	832. INCIPIENT is to BEGINNING as CONGRUOUS is to (A) irrelevant (B) compatible (C) reflexive (D) congregated (E) correlated
884. E	885. PISTOL : TRIGGER :: (A) sword : holster (B) gun : race (C) motor : switch (D) dynamo : amperes (E) rifle : sight
937. B	938. IGNOMINY : DISLOYALTY :: (A) fame : heroism (B) castigation : praise (C) death : victory (D) approbation : consecration
990. B	991. GAZELLE : SWIFT :: (A) horse : slow (B) wolf : sly (C) swan : graceful (D) elephant : gray
1043. C	1044. SATURNINE : MERCURIAL :: (A) Saturn : Venus (B) Appenines : Alps (C) redundant : wordy (D) allegro : adagio
1096. C	1097. ORANGE : MARMALADE :: (A) potato : vegetable (B) jelly : jam (C) tomato : ketchup (D) cake : picnic
1149. B	1150. BANISH : APOSTATE (A) punish : traitor (B) request : assistance (C) welcome : ally (D) avoid : truce
1202. C	1203. MONEY ORDER : POST OFFICE (A) stamp : letter (B) business : government (C) state : federal (D) check : bank
1255. B	1256. LATITUDE : CLIMATE as LONGITUDE : (A) weather (B) time (C) length (D) solstice
1308. D	1309. CHLOROPHYLL : (A) gum (B) ether (C) Erin (D) Chloe as PURITY : WHITE
1361. C	1362. OBSTRUCT is to IMPEDE as IMPENETRABLE is to (A) forebearing (B) hidden (C) impervious (D) merciful

37. C	38. PIT is to PEACH as SUN is to (A) planet (B) moon (C) orbit (D) solar system
90. B	91. DISMAY is to DAUNT as INVOLVE is to (A) turn (B) detract (C) ensnare (D) revolt
143. B	144. GUN is to CLUB as HOUSE is to (A) prehistoric (B) cave (C) cannon (D) rampage
196. C	197. BEACON is to WARNING as SIREN is to (A) stillness (B) warning (C) ships (D) storm
249. A	250. HOSPITAL is to NURSE as SCHOOL is to (A) lawyer (B) apple (C) test (D) teacher
302. C	303. MIX is to COMBINE as CROWD is to (A) team (B) navy (C) football (D) coherence
355. A	356. ACCORD is to BREACH as CONNECTION is to (A) tie (B) dissociation (C) association (D) distrust
408. A	409. CONNOISSEUR is to MASTERPIECE as GOURMET is to (A) food (B) caviar (C) critic (D) gourmand
461. C	462. SPONTANEOUS is to CALCULATED as IMPROMPTU is to (A) ad lib (B) memorized (C) verbose (D) prolific
514. A	515. OFFICE is to DESK as ROOM is to (A) space (B) wallpaper (C) apartment (D) furniture
567. B	568. DRINK is to THIRST as SECURITY is to (A) assuredness (B) stocks (C) terror (D) money
620. D	621. BONDAGE is to SLAVERY as LIBERTY is to (A) country (B) freedom (C) citizen (D) bell
673. A	674. FISH is to FIN as BIRD is to (A) wing (B) five (C) feet (D) beak (E) feathers

726. D	727. QUARREL is to ENEMY as AGREE is to (A) friend (B) disagree (C) agreeable (D) foe
779. E	780. GAUDY is to OSTENTATIOUS as DEJECTED is to (A) oppressed (B) inform (C) rejected (D) depressed (E) determined
832. B	833. INHALE is to LUNG as PERSPIRE is to (A) body (B) heat (C) sweat (D) pore (E) skein
885. C	886. CUBE : PYRAMID :: (A) circle : triangle (B) France : Egypt (C) square : triangle (D) cylinder : trylon (E) hill : right angle
938. A	939. AFFIRM : HINT :: (A) say : deny (B) assert : allege (C) confirm : reject (D) charge : insinuate
991. C	992. THROW : BALL :: (A) kill : bullet (B) shoot : gun (C) question : answer (D) hit : run
1044. D	1045. SPEEDY : GREYHOUND (A) innocent : lamb (B) sluggish : sloth (C) voracious : tiger (D) clever : fox
1097. C	1098. TRIANGLE : PYRAMID :: (A) cone : circle (B) corner : angle (C) tube : cylinder (D) square : box
1150. C	1151. CIRCLE : SPHERE :: (A) square : triangle (B) balloon : jet plane (C) heaven : hell (D) wheel : orange
1203. D	1204. COPPER : PENNY :: (A) policeman : club (B) silver : dime (C) tin : brass (D) nickel : cent
1256. B	1257. ACHILLES : (A) heel (B) spear (C) victory (D) war as SAMSON : HAIR
1309. C	1310. REACTIONARY : RADICAL as HEAVEN : (A) capitalist (B) reduction (C) purgatory (D) religion
1362. C	1363. FELICITY is to BLISS as CONGENIAL is to (A) clever (B) compatible (C) fierce (D) unfriendly

38. D	39. SLICE is to LOAF as ISLAND is to (A) land (B) archipelago (C) peninsula (D) ocean
91. C	92. FEDERAL is to NATION as MUNICIPAL is to (A) city (B) building (C) government (D) mayor
144. B	145. K. CHARACTERISTIC RELATIONSHIP (Frames 146-153)
197. B	198. STEERING WHEEL is to AUTO as RUDDER is to (A) oar (B) boat (C) sail (D) bilge
250. D	251. VIEW is to SCENE as HEAR is to (A) taste (B) concert (C) odor (D) color
303. A	304. STRANGE is to SURPRISE as TERRIBLE is to (A) envy (B) amazement (C) fear (D) ecstasy
356. B	357. BEGINNING is to CREATION as DESTRUCTION is to (A) formation (B) development (C) action (D) cataclysm
409. A	410. INDIGENT is to WEALTHY as GAUCHE is to (A) clumsy (B) clandestine (C) graceful (D) lugubrious
462. B	463. LAY is to LIES as ATE is to (A) eaten (B) eats (C) eating (D) eat
515. D	516. FACULTY is to UNIVERSITY as STAFF is to (A) interne (B) stretcher (C) beds (D) hospital
568. C	569. BALLET is to TERPSICHORE as POETRY is to (A) Zeus (B) Achilles (C) Mt. Olympus (D) Erato
621. B	622. INFLAME is to APPEASE as LAUGH is to (A) cry (B) die (C) joke (D) comedy
674. A	675. INCH is to SQUARE INCH as SQUARE INCH is to (A) inch (B) cubic inch (C) foot (D) yard (E) cube

727. A	728. RAZOR is to SHARP as HOE is to (A) bury (B) dull (C) cuts (D) tree
780. D	781. SALT is to MINE as MARBLE is to (A) palace (B) engraving (C) stone (D) quarry (E) sapphire
833. D	834. TALE is to SUPPOSITION as HISTORY is to (A) reality (B) war (C) peace (D) geography
886. C	887. PROFIT : SELLING :: (A) cost : price (B) fame : bravery (C) praying : loving (D) medal : service (E) work : money
939. D	940. OPEN : SECRETIVE :: (A) mystery : detective (B) tunnel : toll (C) forthright : snide (D) better : best
992. B	993. 36 : 4 :: (A) 3 : 27 (B) 9 : 1 (C) 4 : 12 (D) 12 : 4
1045. B	1046. IMPEACH : DISMISS :: (A) arraign : convict (B) exonerate : charge (C) imprison : jail (D) plant : reap
1098. D	1099. GERM : DISEASE :: (A) trichinosis : pork (B) men : woman (C) doctor : medicine (D) war : destruction
1151. D	1152. WAVE : CREST :: (A) pinnacle : nadir (B) mountain : peak (C) sea : ocean (D) breaker : swimming
1204. B	1205. HIGHWAY : AUTOMOBILE :: (A) sidewalk : pedestrian (B) toll booth : coin (C) wagon : car (D) street : cleaner
1257. A	1258. (A) New York (B) Albany (C) city (D) map : LITTLE ROCK as SACRAMENTO : HELENA
1310. C	1311. VOLCANOES : TOMATOES as (A) bassos (B) dynamos (C) heroes (D) solos: EMBARGOES
1363. B	1364. CAUTIOUS is to CIRCUMSPECT as PRECIPITOUS is to (A) deep (B) flat (C) high (D) steep

39. B	40. HAND is to BODY as STAR is to (A) sky (B) universe (C) eye (D) movie
92. A	93. BELLICOSE is to WARLIKE as PITHY is to (A) pitty (B) extreme (C) succinct (D) pure
	146. RICH is to OWN as WISE is to (A) know (B) teach (C) divulge (D) save
198. B	199. LEATHER is to CALF as WOOL is to (A) clothing (B) tweed (C) sheep (D) skein
251. B	252. PEACE is to WAR as CALM is to (A) tranquillity (B) fight (C) storm (D) noise
304. C	305. TAILOR is to PATTERN as ARCHITECT is to (A) house (B) drawing board (C) plan (D) artist
357. D	358. SWORD is to DUELIST as PEN is to (A) writer (B) ink (C) point (D) inkwell
410. C	411. MAGNANIMITY is to PARSIMONY as TOLERANCE is to (A) advocation (B) totality (C) urgency (D) bigotry
463. B	464. HE is to HIM as WE is to (A) me (B) us (C) them (D) you
516. D	517. LIBRARY is to BOOKS as BANK is to (A) banker (B) money (C) loans (D) finance
569. D	570. THIS is to THAT as HERE is to (A) near (B) their (C) distance (D) there
622. A	623. DORSAL FIN is to TROUT as MANE is to (A) jungle (B) lion (C) forest (D) fish
675. B	676. SOLUTION is to MYSTERY as LEARNING is to (A) study (B) comics (C) college (D) school (E) detective

728. B	729. WINTER is to SUMMER as COLD is to (A) freeze (B) warm (C) wet (D) January
781. D	782. BRICK is to BUILDING as LEATHER is to (A) steer (B) hide (C) belt (D) horse (E) calf
834. A	835. DUKE is to DUCHESS as NUN is to (A) convent (B) priest (C) monk (D) holy (E) religion
887. B	888. BINDING : BOOK :: (A) welding : tank (B) chair : table (C) wire : lamp (D) pencil : paper (E) glue : plate
940. C	941. CONTROL : ORDER :: (A) discipline : school (B) teacher : pupil (C) disorder : climax (D) anarchy : chaos
993. B	994. WOOD : CARVE :: (A) trees : sway (B) paper : burn (C) clay : mold (D) pipe : blow
1046. B	1047. STATE : BORDER :: (A) nation : state (B) flag : loyalty (C) property : fence (D) Idaho : Montana
1099. D	1100. SOLDIER : REGIMENT :: (A) navy : army (B) lake : river (C) star : constellation (D) amphibian : frog
1152. B	1153. APOGEE : PERIGEE (A) inappropriate : apposite (B) opposite : composite (C) paradoxical : incredible (D) effigy : statue
1205. A	1206. CHICKEN : DOG :: (A) cat : mouse (B) hen : pen (C) bark : cackle (D) coop : kennel
1258. B	1259. STRAIGHT : POKER as (A) hit (B) strike (C) dugout (D) manager : BASEBALL
1311. C	1312. AIN'T : SCRAM as LOONEY : (A) scramble (B) moon (C) melon (D) payola
1364. D	1365. INQUISITIVE is to INCURIOUS as MANIFEST is to (A) latent (B) many-sided (C) obvious (D) manipulated

40. B	41. RETINA is to EYE as PISTON is to (A) car (B) engine (C) trunk (D) carburetor
93. C	94. INTEMPERATE is to ABSTEMIOUS as SOMBER is to (A) sleepy (B) jaunty (C) rhythmic (D) soupy
146. A	147. DOVE is to PEACE as BEAVER is to (A) coat (B) industry (C) fur (D) mammal
199. C	200. HAT is to BAND as DRESS is to (A) hem (B) button (C) sleeve (D) belt
252. C	253. HEAD is to HAT as FOOT is to (A) toe (B) leg (C) anatomy (D) shoe
305. C	306. REFEREE is to RULES as CONSCIENCE is to (A) thought (B) regulations (C) morals (D) Freud
358. A	359. STEAM is to WATER as WATER is to (A) heat (B) molecules (C) ice (D) matter
411. D	412. NIGGARDLY is to STINGY as ANGRY is to (A) irascible (B) lethargic (C) pedantic (D) dogmatic
464. B	465. MINER is to SIGNER as LINGER is to (A) stay (B) longer (C) uphold (D) finger
517. B	518. WOLVES is to PACK as CATTLE is to (A) farmer (B) cow (C) field (D) herd
570. D	571. BANANA is to BUNCH as FISH is to (A) aquarium (B) school (C) pond (D) shark
623. B	624. 27 is to 9 as 3 is to (A) 0 (B) 12 (C) 1 (D) 18
676. A	677. ALUMNUS is to ALUMNA as PRINCE is to (A) castle (B) king (C) knight (D) country (E) princess

729. B	730. RUDDER is to SHIP as TAIL is to (A) sail (B) bird (C) dog (D) cat
782. C	783. BASS is to LOW as SOPRANO is to (A) intermediate (B) feminine (C) alto (D) eerie (E) high
835. C	836. **UNIT THREE: COLLEGE BOARD ANALOGY QUESTIONS** (Frames 837-1211) Directions: Select the lettered pair of words which are related in the same way as the capitalized words are related to each other.
888. A	889. DENTIST : CAVITY :: (A) library : books (B) books : study (C) library : knowledge (D) knowledge : school (E) doctor : disease
941. D	942. ASYLUM : REFUGEE :: (A) destination: traveler (B) peace : war (C) lunatic : insanity (D) accident : injury
994. C	995. WORRIED : HYSTERICAL :: (A) hot : cold (B) happy : ecstatic (C) peeved : bitter (D) frozen : cold
1047. C	1048. WORD : CHARADE :: (A) phrase : act (B) idea : philosophy (C) fun : party (D) message : code
1100. C	1101. PLAYER : TEAM :: (A) fawn : doe (B) book : story (C) ball : bat (D) fish : school
1153. A	1154. BANANA : BUNCH :: (A) city : state (B) world : earth (C) president : nation (D) people : continent
1206. D	1207. FLUE : SMOKE (A) chimney : house (B) stove : heat (C) liquid : siphon (D) flame : fire
1259. A	1260. (A) clap (B) play (C) doom (D) fork : MOOD as SLEEK : KEELS
1312. D	1313. AFFECT : EFFECT as (A) influence (B) compose (C) touch (D) infect : RESULT
1365. D	1366. ADUMBRATE is to FORESHADOW as DECLINE is to (A) increase (B) decrease (C) stultify (D) stupefy

41. B	42. PAGE is to BOOK as WORD is to (A) period (B) page (C) novel (D) library
94. B	95. DEVIOUS is to CIRCUITOUS as YIELDING is to (A) yodeling (B) wielding (C) simmering (D) submissive
147. B	148. DETECTIVE is to CLUES as SCIENTIST is to (A) chemicals (B) books (C) experiments (D) facts
200. D	201. SHIP is to MUTINY as ARMY is to (A) court-martial (B) desertion (C) officer (D) navy
253. D	254. SHEEP is to LAMB as DOG is to (A) bone (B) bark (C) pup (D) kennel
306. C	307. BABY is to CARRIAGE as MAN is to (A) woman (B) automobile (C) child (D) adult
359. C	560. CHINESE is to MONGOLIAN as ENGLISH is to (A) Danish (B) race (C) Caucasian (D) language
412. A	413. DERISION is to ENCORE as CATCALL is to (A) oblivion (B) meow (C) acceptance (D) backyard
465. D	466. LIBRETTO is to OPERA as POEM is to (A) edition (B) novel (C) song (D) scenario
518. D	519. TRAVELER is to TRUNK as HOBO is to (A) knapsack (B) vagrant (C) park (D) slum
571. B	572. ACORN is to OAK as INFANT is to (A) individual (B) baby (C) adult (D) male
624. C	625. COSTLY is to SCARCE as CHEAP is to (A) abundant (B) tinny (C) difficult (D) puny
677. E	678. GANDER is to GOOSE as BULL is to (A) cow (B) hog (C) pig (D) lamb (E) reap

730. B	731. GRANARY is to WHEAT as LIBRARY is to (A) desk (B) books (C) paper (D) librarian
783. E	784. MASK is to FACE as HELMET is to (A) steel (B) head (C) combat (D) duel (E) football
	837. ISLAND : OCEAN :: (A) pit : orange (B) filament : bulb (C) city : nation (D) water: oasis (E) pine : grove
889. E	890. COKE : COAL :: (A) bread : eat (B) money : work (C) bread : dough (D) coal : rubber (E) dough : wheat
942. A	943. MOTH : CLOTHING :: (A) egg : larva (B) suit : dress (C) hole : repair (D) stigma : reputation
995. B	996. LINCOLN : NEBRASKA :: (A) Washington : D.C. (B) Trenton : New Jersey (C) New York : U.S. (D) Chicago : New York
1048. D	1049. BUZZ : HUM :: (A) noise : explosion (B) reverberation : peal (C) tinkle : clang (D) echo : sound
1101. D	1102. BOXER : GLOVES :: (A) swimmer : water (B) librarian : glasses (C) businessman : bills (D) bacteriologist : microscope
1154. A	1155. DECISION : CONSIDERATION :: (A) gift : party (B) plea : request (C) greed : charity (D) fulfillment : wish
1207. C	1208. WATER : OAR :: (A) sea : island (B) boat : canoe (C) lake : paddle (D) earth : shovel
1260. C	1261. CONTUMELY : (A) delight (B) eulogy (C) apparel (D) reproof as CONVEX : CONCAVE
1313. A	1314. (A) saliva (B) oil (C) motor (D) comb : COGWHEEL as GEAR : MOUTH
1366. B	1367. FETISH is to TALISMAN as FEALTY is to (A) allegiance (B) faithlessness (C) payment (D) real estate

42. B	43. STATE is to COUNTRY as CONTINENT is to (A) world (B) globe (C) country (D) city
95. D	96. ORIGINATE is to INVENT as COPY is to (A) song (B) imitate (C) study (D) work
148. D	149. COMMON is to IRON as RARE is to (A) steak (B) crowd (C) humor (D) diamond
201. B	202. WEIGHT is to OUNCE as DISTANCE is to (A) ruler (B) yard (C) runner (D) arithmetic
254. C	255. SUMMER is to SWIMMING as WINTER is to (A) flying (B) skating (C) burning (D) holiday
307. B	308. LEAVE is to STAY as DEPART is to (A) home (B) abide (C) run (D) sleep
360. C	361. DIAGNOSIS is to ANALYSIS as THESIS is to (A) college (B) research (C) library (D) paper
413. C	414. SHEEP is to EWE as ALUMNUS is to (A) alumna (B) alumni (C) alum (D) alumnas
466. C	467. HYPOCRISY is to HONESTY as HOSTILITY is to (A) war (B) amity (C) hospital (D) hostage
519. A	520. REQUEST is to DEMAND as VISIT is to (A) return (B) welcome (C) invasion (D) house
572. C	573. LAUD is to DEGRADE as PRAISE is to (A) victory (B) enjoyment (C) criticize (D) succeed
625. A	626. VITAMINS is to DISEASE as FOOD is to (A) health (B) death (C) coffin (D) drink
678. A	679. BLANCHES is to PALLOR as INSTITUTES is to (A) form (B) sum (C) purpose (D) beginning (E) cataract

731. B	732. INTELLIGENCE is to UNDERSTANDING as STUPIDITY is to (A) ignorance (B) pleasure (C) school (D) unhappiness
784. B	785. FINGER is to TACTILE as NOSE is to (A) proboscis (B) smell (C) olfactory (D) redolent (E) perfume
837. D	838. FRUIT : ORCHARD :: (A) tree : forest (B) fish : sea (C) lumber : mill (D) seed : flower (E) money : cash
890. C	891. INDIAN : AMERICA :: (A) Hindu : Indian (B) wetback : Mexico (C) soil : land (D) magic : India (E) Hindu : India
943. D	944. DELUSION : MIRAGE :: (A) haunter : specter (B) imagination : concentration (C) dream : reality (D) mirror : glass
996. B	997. FRANCE : EUROPE :: (A) Australia : New Zealand (B) Paris : France (C) Israel : Egypt (D) Algeria : Africa
1049. C	1050. INSULT : INVULNERABLE :: (A) success : capable (B) poverty : miserable (C) purchase : refundable (D) assault : impregnable
1102. D	1103. POISON : DEATH :: (A) book : pages (B) music : violin (C) kindness : cooperation (D) life : famine
1155. D	1156. ROCK : SLATE :: (A) wave : sea (B) boat : kayak (C) swimmer : male (D) lifeguard : beach
1208. D	1209. ENERGY : STRENGTH :: (A) peace : negotiation (B) fun : laughter (C) enjoyment : riches (D) loss : compensation
1261. B	1262. WINDOW : CURTAIN as (A) linen (B) hole (C) house (D) table: CLOTH
1314. D	1315. **UNIT FIVE: ANALOGIES REQUIRING A GOOD VOCABULARY** (Frames 1316-1377)
1367. A	1368. INDUCTILE is to INDOMITABLE as SEJANT is to (A) reticent (B) remarkable (C) sojourning (D) sitting

96. B	97. LEXICON is to DICTIONARY as OFFICER is to (A) policeman (B) law (C) protection (D) crime
149. D	150. MISER is to MONEY as HYPOCHONDRIAC is to (A) complaining (B) weakness (C) insistence (D) health
202. B	203. DOWAGER is to DEBUTANTE as AGE is to (A) years (B) old (C) youth (D) era
255. B	256. SCARCITY is to PLENTY as STEAM is to (A) water (B) fury (C) heat (D) ice
308. B	309. PONDER is to DECIDE as DISCUSS is to (A) argue (B) debate (C) conclude (D) vacillation
361. B	362. EASY is to HARD as SIMPLE is to (A) complex (B) dimple (C) sententious (D) Simon
414. A	415. MOOSE is to MOOSE as I is to (A) me (B) they (C) us (D) we
467. B	468. LATITUDE is to LONGITUDE as AXIS is to (A) origin (B) axis (C) degrees (D) vertical
520. C	521. SAFE is to COMBINATION as DOOR is to (A) lintel (B) watchman (C) door mat (D) key
573. C	574. FOREMAN is to FACTORY as PRINCPAL is to (A) bank (B) tools (C) supervisor (D) school
626. B	627. 25 is to 5 as 16 is to (A) 4 (B) 12 (C) 20 (D) 1
679. D	680. TALKING is to YELLING as DANCING is to (A) rejoicing (B) mixing (C) prancing (D) singing (E) slinging

732. A	733. SAND is to GLASS as CLAY is to (A) stone (B) hay (C) bricks (D) dirt
785. C	786. PORPOISE is to SEA as MOLE is to (A) forest (B) ground (C) air (D) cliff (E) tree
838. B	839. ALTITUDE : MOUNTAIN :: (A) height : weight (B) depth : ocean (C) mass : energy (D) latitude : country (E) incline : hill
891. E	892. WEALTH : MERCENARY :: (A) fame : soldier (B) love : mother (C) poverty : crime (D) gold : South Africa (E) gold : Midas
944. A	945. LAW : CITIZEN :: (A) democracy : communism (B) weapon : peace (C) reins : horse (D) gangster : policeman
997. D	998. JOY : ECSTASY :: (A) admiration : love (B) weather : humidity (C) happiness : sorrow (D) life : hope
1050. D	1051. LARCENY : GRAND :: (A) theft : daring (B) school : elementary (C) pepper : bitter (D) silence : peaceful
1103. C	1104. ANTISEPTIC : GERMS :: (A) bullet : death (B) mosquitos : disease (C) lion : prey (D) doctor : medicine
1156. B	1157. HORSE : RIDE :: (A) sharpener : sharpen (B) purchase : make (C) use : reuse (D) break : crack
1209. B	1210. FABRIC : FIBERS :: (A) cloth : wool (B) dress : dressmaker (C) blood : veins (D) brick : clay
1262. D	1263. (A) quantity (B) ream (C) tree (D) news: PAPER as DOZEN : EGGS
1315.	1316. FULMINATION is to TRINITROTOLUENE as DISSIPATION is to (A) tyranny (B) gluttony (C) concentration (D) desire
1368. D	1369. HECKLE is to NEEDLE as REPLENISH is to (A) stock (B) frame (C) book (D) plan

45. NEPHEW is to NIECE
as UNCLE is to
(A) man (B) relative (C) father (D) aunt

| 97. A | **98.** H. ANTONYM RELATIONSHIP (Frames 99-113) |

150. A

151. AUDIBLE is to NOISE
as VISIBLE is to
(A) picture (B) honesty (C) distance (D) heaven

203. C

204. CALF is to SHOE
as GOOSE is to
(A) gander (B) pillow (C) roast (D) feathers

256. D

257. TREE is to BARK
as BODY is to
(A) voice (B) skin (C) hands (D) height

309. C

310. CAR is to MECHANIC
as MAN is to
(A) doctor (B) butcher (C) house (D) lawyer

362. A

363. MEAT is to FORK
as SOUP is to
(A) restaurant (B) cook (C) spoon (D) napkin

415. D

416. DONKEY is to DONKEYS
as MOUSE is to
(A) mouses (B) mice (C) rats (D) trap

468. B

469. WAGES is to LABOR
as PROFIT is to
(A) sales (B) investment (C) management (D) interest

521. D

522. SCOTLAND is to BAGPIPE
as SPAIN is to
(A) harp (B) guitar (C) piano (D) trumpet

574. D

575. INCH is to MILE
as HUT is to
(A) foundation (B) skyscraper (C) building (D) abode

627. A

628. THIRST is to WATER
as HUNGER is to
(A) starving (B) eat (C) drink (D) food

680. C

681. REVERT is to REVERSION
as SYMPATHIZE is to   (A) sympathic
(B) symposium (C) sympathy (D) sympathizer (E) simplicity

733. C	**734.** DISLOYAL is to FAITHLESS as IMPERFECTION is to (A) contamination (B) depression (C) foible (D) decrepitude
786. B	**787.** REGISTER is to ENROLL as REGALE is to (A) endure (B) remain (C) feast (D) cohere (E) storm
839. B	**840.** SUN : DAY :: (A) moon : dusk (B) blub : house (C) stars : night (D) heat : summer (E) earth : axis
892. E	**893.** BOTTLE : BRITTLE :: (A) tire : elastic (B) rubber : opaque (C) iron : strong (D) glass : transparent (E) chair : comfortable
945. C	**946.** MYSTERY : CLUE :: (A) key : door (B) fruit : bowl (C) test : study (D) detective : crime
998. A	**999.** PENCIL : SHARPEN :: (A) knife : cut (B) carpenter : build (C) wood : saw (D) well : fill
1051. B	**1052.** GARBAGE : SQUALOR :: (A) filth : cleanliness (B) fame : knowledge (C) diamonds : magnificence (D) color : brush
1104. C	**1105.** MYTH : STORY :: (A) fiction : reality (B) bonnet : hat (C) literature : poetry (D) flower : redness
1157. B	**1158.** DUNCE : CLEVER :: (A) idiot : stupid (B) courage : fearful (C) help : weak (D) worry : poor
1210. D	**1211.** STUFFING : CUSHION :: (A) nose : face (B) cat : whiskers (C) water : pipe (D) turkey : course
1263. B	**1264.** HEBREW : TALMUD as GREEK : (A) Parthenon (B) Republic (C) Aristotle (D) nation
1316. B	**1317.** EDIFICATION is to AWARENESS as EXACERBATION is to (A) soreness (B) excitement (C) reduction (D) deliberation
1369. A	**1370.** KINETIC is to MOTION as PISCATORIAL is to (A) pizza (B) painting (C) fish (D) lip

45. D	46. HAND is to ELBOW as FOOT is to (A) muscle (B) knee (C) leg (D) toe
	99. SKILLFUL is to CLUMSY as DEFT is to (A) alert (B) awkward (C) dumb (D) rough
151. A	152. PILOT is to ALERT as MARKSMAN is to (A) strong (B) cruel (C) kind (D) steady
204. B	205. TRANSITORY is to ETERNAL as SECULAR is to (A) profane (B) irreverent (C) religious (D) blasphemous
257. B	258. END is to BEGIN as ABOLISH is to (A) establish (B) finish (C) tyranny (D) crusade
310. A	311. ARMY is to RECRUIT as RELIGION is to (A) priest (B) worshiper (C) convert (D) church
363. C	364. SPEECH is to MAN as SONG is to (A) ditty (B) bird (C) sheep (D) tune
416. B	417. AGENT is to COMMISSIONS as AUTHOR is to (A) royalties (B) charges (C) fees (D) contributions
469. C	470. RUST is to IRON as MOLD is to (A) bread (B) penicillin (C) virus (D) disease
522. B	523. GRAMMAR is to LANGUAGE as ALGEBRA is to (A) geometry (B) school (C) classroom (D) mathematics
575. B	576. BUD is to FLOWER as SCRATCH is to (A) thorn (B) scar (C) amputation (D) fever
628. D	629. SECOND is to FOURTH as B is to (A) A (B) D (C) Q (D) C
681. C	682. DOWN is to DOWNY as AGE is to (A) aging (B) old (C) ancient (D) historic (E) stagnant

734. C	735. TEARS is to SORROW as LAUGHTER is to (A) joy (B) smile (C) girls (D) grain
787. C	788. SARDONIC is to IRONICAL as SUBVERSIVE is to (A) instructive (B) destructive (C) influential (D) subterranean (E) inane
840. C	841. FOREST : FLORA :: (A) zoo : animals (B) jungle : fauna (C) countryside : cows (D) orchard : trees (E) vase : flowers
893. A	894. ELEPHANT : TUSK :: (A) camel : hump (B) leopard : skin (C) knight : spear (D) snake : fangs (E) desk : top
946. C	947. DUNE : WIND :: (A) fan : flame (B) ignorance : bliss (C) sky : cloud (D) delta : water
999. C	1000. APPLE : BANANA :: (A) milk : meat (B) Monday : Tuesday (C) pear : apricot (D) egg : fish
1052. C	1053. PLEA : UNYIELDING :: (A) call : interested (B) reply : rejected (C) appeal : adamant (D) remark : confused
1105. B	1106. HARASSMENT : ANGER :: (A) disappointment : sorrow (B) height : weight (C) laughter : tears (D) marriage : love
1158. B	1159. EAST : WEST :: (A) south : east (B) left : right (C) direction : correction (D) opposite : antonymn
1211. A	1212. **UNIT FOUR: MILLER ANALOGY TEST (Sample)** Directions: Select the lettered choice which completes the relationship. (Frames 1213-1314)
1264. B	1265. (A) 16 (B) 3^2 (C) 21.5 D. 2-1/2 : 4^2 as .2 : 1/5
1317. A	1318. GASTRONOMICAL is to GOURMET as GEOLOGICAL is to (A) raconteur (B) entomologist (C) etymologist (D) paleontologist
1370. C	1371. REPUGN is to COMPROMISE as RESCIND is to (A) refuse (B) rest (C) decipher (D) validate

46. B	47. MATURITY is to ADOLESCENCE as CHILDHOOD is to (A) manhood (B) infancy (C) school (D) immaturity
99. B	100. ATHEIST is to RELIGION as PACIFIST is to (A) peace (B) ocean (C) hate (D) war
152. D	153. LADY is to LADYLIKE as MAN is to (A) gentlemanly (B) male (C) manly (D) mannish
205. C	206. ORIGINATE is to IMITATE as INVENT is to (A) copy (B) telephone (C) replica (D) devise
258. A	259. COPPER is to ORE as MARBLE is to (A) granite (B) hardness (C) limestone (D) sculpture
311. C	312. DOOR is to BOLT as LETTER is to (A) envelope (B) pen (C) seal (D) paper
364. B	365. MAN is to BREAD as HORSE is to (A) stable (B) duck (C) barn (D) hay
417. A	418. DENTIST is to CAVITY as POLICEMAN is to (A) convict (B) justice (C) conduct (D) crime
470. A	471. ORIGINAL is to COPY as GENUINE is to (A) diamond (B) imitation (C) legal (D) reputable
523. D	524. GASOLINE is to FUEL as OIL is to (A) car (B) train (C) lubricant (D) motor
576. B	577. POD is to PEA as COB is to (A) farmer (B) kernel (C) silo (D) food
629. B	630. GENERAL is to ARMY as MAYOR is to (A) city (B) navy (C) state (D) country
682. B	683. I is to MINE as MAN is to (A) men (B) his (C) man's (D) mine (E) its

735. A	736. COLD is to ICE as HEAT is to (A) lightning (B) warm (C) steam (D) coat
788. B	789. CLOCK is to HOUR as BAROMETER is to (A) gale (B) weather (C) rain (D) pressure (E) air
841. D	842. IGNORANCE : BOOKS :: (A) study : learning (B) school : teacher (C) candy : store (D) darkness : lamps (E) publication : fame
894. D	895. CAUSEWAY : BRIDGE :: (A) swamp : stream (B) viaduct : land (C) bridge : river (D) train : road (E) low : high
947. D	948. SPEAK : STUTTER :: (A) walk : limp (B) find : grope (C) yell : silence (D) cry : laugh
1000. C	1001. WATER : BOIL :: (A) bed : sleep (B) food : drink (C) song : sing (D) violin : string
1053. C	1054. REBELLION : CRUSH :: (A) revolution : discourage (B) riot : quell (C) revolt : plot (D) insurgency : detect
1106. A	1107. VERB : SUBJECT :: (A) child : book (B) cup : glass (C) hand : body (D) action : thing
1159. B	1160. CELLS : TISSUE :: (A) singer : choir (B) crowd : person (C) organs : system (D) tissue : box
1212.	1213. WHEEL : FENDER as PROPELLER : (A) plane (B) wing (C) airport (D) beam
1265. A	1266. (A) revision (B) respite (C) continuation (D) appraisal : ESTIMATE as DIVULGE : DISCLOSE
1318. D	1319. ECUMENICAL is to CHURCH as CULINARY is to (A) bedroom (B) closet (C) knife (D) kitchen
1371. D	1372. ELAND is to HORNS as REPTILE is to (A) vertebrate (B) zoology (C) animal (D) fangs

47. **B**	**48.** THEODORE is to TED as ELEANOR is to (A) Dorothy (B) girl (C) beauty (D) Nell
100. **D**	**101.** FLOOD is to LEVEE as RAIN is to (A) cloud (B) sunshine (C) umbrella (D) forecast
153. **A**	**154. L. SEQUENCE RELATIONSHIP** (Frames 155-160)
206. **A**	**207.** ROOM is to WINDOW as HEAD is to (A) body (B) chief (C) tail (D) eye
259. **C**	**260.** DEPRESSION is to DESPAIR as CHEER is to (A) victory (B) hope (C) gloom (D) celebration
312. **C**	**313.** DIVIDE is to MULTIPLY as SUBTRACT is to (A) add (B) algebra (C) number (D) arithmetic
365. **D**	**366.** OBEY is to COMMAND as PRIVATE is to (A) officer (B) marine (C) office (D) war
418. **D**	**419.** COFFEE is to BEAN as TOBACCO is to (A) cigarette (B) smoke (C) leaf (D) bush
471. **B**	**472.** MEDLEY is to ONE as MISCELLANEOUS is to (A) collective (B) undetermined (C) righteous (D) single
524. **C**	**525.** SILK is to RAYON as BUTTER is to (A) margarine (B) oil (C) cream (D) bread
577. **B**	**578.** WORD is to SENTENCE as PARAGRAPH is to (A) story (B) punctuation (C) title (D) poem
630. **A**	**631.** VERB is to NOUN as PREDICATE is to (A) preposition (B) adjective (C) subject (D) phrase
683. **C**	**684.** DISLOYAL is to FAITHLESS as IMPERFECTION is to (A) contamination (B) depression (C) foible (D) decrepitude (E) praise

736. C	737. REMUNERATIVE is to PROFITABLE as FRAUDULENT is to (A) lying (B) slander (C) fallacious (D) plausible (E) reward
789. D	790. BARREL is to WINE as SILO is to (A) horses (B) floss (C) grain (D) refuse (E) ashes
842. D	843. AILMENT : DOCTOR :: (A) medicine : pharmacist (B) care : relief (C) victim : crime (D) fire : water (E) war : victory
895. A	896. HACK : DRIVER :: (A) buggy : horse (B) army : captain (C) machine : operator (D) tug : pilot (E) school : teacher
948. A	949. MATURITY : WISDOM :: (A) simplicity : complication (B) youth : folly (C) drama : comedy (D) vegetable fruit
1001. C	1002. GHANDI : CAESAR :: (A) Washington : Roosevelt (B) Lincoln : McKinley (C) Newton : Galileo (D) Napoleon : Pershing
1054. B	1055. BANAL : UNIQUE :: (A) scintillating : simple (B) restless : tireless (C) leftist : radical (D) ruthless : murderous
1107. D	1108. FINGER : HAND :: (A) arm : sleeve (B) shoe : foot (C) strand : hair (D) blouse : skirt
1160. C	1161. DISTRUST : MENDACITY :: (A) remove : doubt (B) fear : truculence (C) break : back (D) warm : enemy
1213. B	1214. BRIDGE : TUNNEL as (A) zodiac (B) constellation (C) zenith (D) galaxy : NADIR
1266. D	1267. ITALY : SWITZERLAND as (A) Chile (B) Canada (C) Australia (D) India : PAKISTAN
1319. D	1320. DICHOTOMY is to DIVISION as DISSEMBLE is to (A) feign (B) assemble (C) resemble (D) return
1372. D	1373. QUOIN is to ARCH as TUSSOCK is to (A) hair (B) tusk (C) elephant (D) tuxedo

48. D	49. BARITONE is to TENOR as CONTRALTO is to (A) opera (B) soprano (C) woman (D) song
101. C	102. NOTHING is to EVERYTHING as WHISPER is to (A) mystery (B) yell (C) voice (D) ghost
	155. MAY is to FEBRUARY as NOVEMBER is to (A) August (B) January (C) October (D) July
207. D	208. ALTERATION is to GARMENT as REVISION is to (A) book (B) remodeling (C) correction (D) content
260. B	261. LOVE is to CARESS as ANGER is to (A) strike (B) rage (C) shout (D) threaten
313. A	314. PARTIAL is to DISINTERESTED as BARREN is to (A) noble (B) fruitful (C) distant (D) bearing
366. A	367. ARM is to LEG as FLIPPER is to (A) wing (B) tail (C) head (D) whale
419. C	420. BIRD is to CAGE as CONVICT is to (A) justice (B) warden (C) murdered (D) prison
472. D	473. NOISOME is to FETID as INTREPID is to (A) courageous (B) cowardly (C) quiet (D) boisterous
525. A	526. SALESMAN is to PRODUCT as TEACHER is to (A) principal (B) English (C) pupils (D) subject
578. A	579. PAGE is to BOOK as LEAF is to (A) branch (B) forest (C) brush (D) trunk
631. C	632. HALLOWED is to SACRED as DEPRAVED is to (A) mean (B) corrupt (C) devoted (D) bad
684. C	685. MOHAIR is to GOAT as WOOL is to (A) coat (B) camel (C) sheep (D) horse (E) chair

737. C	738. AX is to WOODSMAN as AWL is to (A) cut (B) hew (C) plumber (D) pierce (E) cobbler
790. C	791. SILK is to FABRIC as TEAK is to (A) flower (B) animal (C) tree (D) metal (E) bird
843. D	844. RETREAT : DEFEAT :: (A) retrench : depression (B) victory : charge (C) stand : death (D) campaign : advance (E) armistice : surrender
896. D	897. CONVEX : CONCAVE :: (A) in : out (B) nose : mouth (C) hill : hole (D) round : square (E) myopia : astigmatism
949. B	950. COWS : MILK :: (A) rats : cheese (B) bees : honey (C) birds : wings (D) cats : dogs
1002. B	1003. DUTCH : HOLLAND :: (A) Algerian : Africa (B) Eiffel Tower : Paris (C) Buckingham Palace : England (D) Flemish : Belgium
1055. A	1056. BIRD : AVIARY :: (A) fish : water (B) bee : apiary (C) lion : jungle (D) worm : earth
1108. C	1109. EXERCISE : REDUCE :: (A) grumble : resign (B) snow : freeze (C) spending : save (D) luck : win
1161. B	1162. PREAMBLE : CONSTITUTION :: (A) introduction : conclusion (B) preview : conclusion (C) prologue : play (D) Bill of Rights : amendment
1214. C	1215. SWALLOWS : (A) Capistrano (B) Bologna (C) Naples (D) Rome as CHICKENS : ROOST
1267. D	1268. APPLE : DESK as (A) loyalty (B) honor (C) health (D) fruit : WOMAN
1320. A	1321. CREPUSCULAR is to INDISTINCT as CURSORY is to (A) profane (B) egregrious (C) superficial (D) unique
1373. A	1374. HORTATORY is to SUBJUNCTIVE as PRESENT is to (A) future (B) indicative (C) grammar (D) past

49. B	50. DAUGHTER is to MOTHER as SON is to (A) child (B) grandfather (C) boy (D) father
102. B	103. ADVANCE is to HALT as PROCEED is to (A) return (B) stop (C) go (D) conquer
155. A	156. THIRD is to FIRST as JEFFERSON is to (A) Washington (B) White House (C) president (D) Napoleon
208. A	209. UNIVERSAL is to LIMITED as INFINITE is to (A) eternal (B) finite (C) incalculable (D) unending
261. A	262. NIECE is to AUNT as NEPHEW is to (A) boy (B) uncle (C) girl (D) father
314. B	315. TASTE is to SWEET as ODOR is to (A) flower (B) rose (C) smell (D) fragrant
367. B	368. SISTER is to FAMILY as CARROT is to (A) tomato (B) salad (C) root (D) vegetable
420. D	421. BIRTH is to DEATH as INTRODUCTION is to (A) salutations (B) lecturer (C) conclusion (D) prologue
473. A	474. PESTLE is to PHARMACIST as STETHOSCOPE is to (A) teacher (B) author (C) physician (D) doctor
526. D	527. SCHOOL is to COLORS as COUNTRY is to (A) flag (B) patriot (C) leader (D) government
579. A	580. BALL is to BASEBALL as HORSESHOE is to (A) anvil (B) blacksmith (C) horseshoes (D) oats
632. B	633. NONE is to LITTLE as NEVER is to (A) frequent (B) often (C) always (D) seldom
685. C	686. MASCULINE is to GENDER as RUBY is to (A) dispute (B) country (C) color (D) argument (E) enemy

738. E	739. SURGEON is to SCALPEL as BUTCHER is to (A) mallet (B) cleaver (C) chisel (D) wrench (E) medicine
791. C	792. POISON is to STRYCHNINE as HUE is to (A) brick (B) grain (C) acid (D) mammal (E) russet
844. A	845. OBLITERATE : PAINT :: (A) earthquake : city (B) write : ink (C) destroy : house (D) drown : water (E) artist : canvas
897. C	898. PRISM : KALEIDOSCOPE :: (A) window : house (B) bottle : glass (C) tool : toy (D) gear : machine (E) sight : play
950. B	951. BOREDOM : DIVERSION (A) travel : ennui (B) pain : narcotic (C) fun : frolic (D) serfdom : conversion
1003. D	1004. GLASSES : READING :: (A) glass : mirror (B) light : vision (C) spoon : fork (D) hand : object
1056. B	1057. PROFICIENCY : MONEY :: (A) profit : money (B) practice : perfection (C) knowledge : study (D) skill : expertness
1109. D	1110. EARTH : VENUS :: (A) star : sun (B) page : book (C) Idaho : Montana (D) time : life
1162. C	1163. GARBAGE : SQUALOR :: (A) filth : cleanliness (B) fame : knowledge (C) diamonds : magnificence (D) color : brush
1215. A	1216. ROUT : TOUR as (A) Mary (B) Sue (C) Ruth (D) Enid : DINE
1268. D	1269. WHO : WHOM as (A) where (B) pronoun (C) syntax (D) subject : COMPLEMENT
1321. C	1322. VIXEN is to SEAMSTRESS as BACCHUS is to (A) Ceres (B) Neptune (C) Venus (D) Minerva
1374. B	1375. INTRACTABLE is to OBEDIENT as RAPACIOUS is to (A) noisy (B) charitable (C) riparian (D) destructive

50. D	51. STRIPES is to SPOTS as ZEBRA is to (A) leopard (B) animal (C) design (D) Africa
103. B	104. BULLDOG is to PEKINESE as EAGLE is to (A) starling (B) flock (C) wing (D) nest
156. A	157. Q is to M as G is to (A) K (B) C (C) D (D) F
209. B	210. CAR is to BUMPER as KNIGHT is to (A) steel (B) man (C) armor (D) charger
262. B	263. HEAR is to SOUND as SEE is to (A) eye (B) sense (C) picture (D) Rembrandt
315. D	316. SCARCE is to RARE as ABUNDANT is to (A) plentiful (B) cheap (C) costly (D) many
368. D	369. PRONG is to FORK as TOOTH is to (A) comb (B) hair (C) teeth (D) finger
421. C	422. FOOTBALL is to SIGNALS as WAR is to (A) guns (B) codes (C) peace (D) soldiers
474. C	475. SENILITY is to CHILDHOOD as DUSK is to (A) twilight (B) dawn (C) night (D) rain
527. A	528. PLAY is to REHEARSAL GAME is to (A) football (B) practice (C) coach (D) players
580. C	581. STUDENT is to CLASS as TILE is to (A) mosaic (B) floor (C) porcelain (D) concrete
633. D	634. CONCERT is to RECORD as LANDSCAPE is to (A) photograph (B) artist (C) countryside (D) tree
686. C	687. SEED is to SOW as EGG is to (A) pollinate (B) hatch (C) plant (D) fruit (E) earth

739. B	740. CAT is to FELINE as HORSE is to (A) equine (B) tiger (C) quadruped (D) carnivorous (E) vulpine
792. E	793. DESSICATE is to MOISTEN as ERECT is to (A) elevate (B) exalt (C) demolish (D) corrode (E) institute
845. B	846. ADMIRATION : CHAMPION :: (A) hate : villain (B) cry : misfortune (C) love : store (D) hero : affection (E) sadness : pity
898. D	899. MARTINET : RIGIDITY (A) soldier : bravery (B) general : philosopher (C) man : boy (D) sergeant : general (E) benefactor : kindness
951. B	952. WINDOW : STORE :: (A) shop : merchant (B) grocery : delicatessen (C) facade : building (D) pane : glass
1004. B	1005. FLAME : BURN :: (A) sun : earth (B) birth : life (C) glass : crack (D) insult : anger
1057. C	1058. NUMISMATIST : COINS :: (A) philatelist : stamps (B) bibliophile : bibles (C) benefactor : kindness (D) monarchist : money
1110. C	1111. EYE : EAR :: (A) boy : girl (B) mouse : house (C) notebook : student (D) shirt : pants
1163. C	1164. CONVICTED : GUILTY :: (A) jailed : incarcerated (B) judged : tried (C) apprehended : guiltless (D) vindicated : innocent
1216. D	1217. (A) walk (B) river (C) home (D) stocking : RUN as TOUCH : DOWN
1269. D	1270. LONGFELLOW : WHITMAN as TENNYSON : (A) Tagore (B) Kipling (C) Heine (D) James
1322. B	1323. GLABROUS is to HIRSUTE as FACTITIOUS is to (A) authentic (B) fictional (C) fluent (D) replete
1375. B	1376. ESKER is to GEOLOGY as PNEUMATICS is to (A) medicine (B) disease (C) physics (D) cars

51. A	52. SEA is to COAST as RIVER is to (A) inlet (B) delta (C) stream (D) bank
104. A	105. LIGHT is to DARK as WET is to (A) snow (B) rain (C) sand (D) dry
157. B	158. ABD is to EFH as IJL is to (A) MNO (B) NOP (C) NOO (D) MNP
210. C	211. ANCHOR is to BOAT as BRAKE is to (A) car (B) wheel (C) stop (D) crack
263. C	264. BEE is to STINGER as MAN is to (A) wound (B) woman (C) fist (D) shield
316. B	317. RISK is to DANGER as CAUTION is to (A) safety (B) carelessness (C) accidents (D) patience
369. A	370. MEDAL is to HERO as PRIZE is to (A) winner (B) fighter (C) monkey (D) package
422. B	423. MINNOW is to HIPPOPOTAMUS as MOUSE is to (A) rodent (B) rat (C) elephant (D) ground
475. B	476. COACH is to PLAYER as TEACHER is to (A) school (B) study (C) ignorance (D) pupil
528. B	529. GUEST is to ACCEPTANCE as HOST is to (A) party (B) hostess (C) refreshments (D) invitation
581. A	582. DOOR is to HOUSE as GATE is to (A) sidewalk (B) yard (C) toll (D) window
634. A	635. ASSAULT is to RIVAL as EMBRACE is to (A) hug (B) love (C) effection (D) ally
687. B	688. CONTEMPORARY is to PRESENT as POSTERITY is to (A) past (B) present (C) modern (D) ancient (E) future

740. A	741. ADVERSITY is to HAPPINESS as VEHEMENCE is to (A) misfortune (B) gayety (C) troublesome (D) petulance (E) serenity
793. C	794. FRAUGHT is to LADEN as FRANK is to (A) ingenuous (B) postal (C) concealed (D) enticing (E) secretive
846. A	847. VICTORY : JUBILATION :: (A) defeat : consternation (B) wedding : felicitation (C) election : celebration (D) downfall : waterfall (E) slavery : emancipation
899. E	900. CADAVER : ANIMAL :: (A) salad : greens (B) corpse : man (C) death : life (D) morgue : jungle (E) life : death
952. C	953. PRIMA DONNA : ARIA (A) opera : metropolitan (B) tragedian : soliloquy (C) ballerina : dance (D) contralto : tenor
1005. D	1006. CAP : BOTTLE :: (A) color : room (B) room : bed (C) color : painting (D) slipcover : sofa
1058. A	1059. ALLEGATION : PROOF :: (A) hypothesis : fact (B) allegiance : loyalty (C) assertion : statement (D) testimony : evidence
1111. D	1112. BOAT : CARGO :: (A) fish : wing (B) basket : rolls (C) teacher : student (D) water : glass
1164. D	1165. FLOUNDER : FISH :: (A) man : suit (B) cat : dog (C) fish : gill (D) antelope : animal
1217. C	1218. BALMY : (A) explosive (B) handy (C) talkative (D) mild FAITHFUL : TRUE
1270. B	1271. WHIP : CRACK as HAVOC : (A) cry (B) destruction (C) yell (D) possession
1323. A	1324. CHOLERIC is to PLACID as BANAL is to (A) portly (B) flippant (C) reasonable (D) unique
1376. C	1377. KAYAK is to DHOW as TOBOGGAN is to (A) chair (B) tram (C) tobacco (D) bog

52. **D**	**53. E. ACTION TO OBJECT RELATIONSHIP** (Frames 54-62)	TURN TO PAGE 1 FOR NEXT QUESTION
105. **D**	**106. DAY is to NIGHT** as SUN is to (A) solar (B) moon (C) universe (D) heat	TURN TO PAGE 1 FOR NEXT QUESTION
158. **D**	**159. TUESDAY is to THURSDAY** as SATURDAY is to (A) Sunday (B) Monday (C) Wednesday (D) Friday	TURN TO PAGE 1 FOR NEXT QUESTION
211. **A**	**212. REMEMBER is to FORGET** as FIND is to (A) locate (B) keep (C) lose (D) return	TURN TO PAGE 1 FOR NEXT QUESTION
264. **C**	**265. HOUSE is to BUILD** as TRENCH is to (A) dig (B) trap (C) obliterate (D) dry	TURN TO PAGE 1 FOR NEXT QUESTION
317. **A**	**318. COPY is to ORIGINATE** as IMITATE is to (A) pretend (B) mimic (C) invent (D) impersonate	TURN TO PAGE 1 FOR NEXT QUESTION
370. **A**	**371. MINNOW is to SHARK** as PUPPY is to (A) elephant (B) whale (C) wolfhound (D) mastodon	TURN TO PAGE 1 FOR NEXT QUESTION
423. **C**	**424. QUARANTINE is to ISOLATION** as QUALM is to (A) misgiving (B) palm (C) quake (D) quarrel	TURN TO PAGE 1 FOR NEXT QUESTION
476. **D**	**477. TREE is to LIMB** as MAN is to (A) hand (B) skin (C) arm (D) head	TURN TO PAGE 1 FOR NEXT QUESTION
529. **D**	**530. PACK is to WOLF** as BUNCH is to (A) animal (B) banana (C) burns (D) lunch	TURN TO PAGE 1 FOR NEXT QUESTION
582. **B**	**583. FEET is to TOE** as HANDS is to (A) body (B) arm (C) back (D) finger	TURN TO PAGE 1 FOR NEXT QUESTION
635. **D**	**636. HASH is to FOOD** as MEDLEY is to (A) play (B) musical (C) music (D) singer	TURN TO PAGE 1 FOR NEXT QUESTION
688. **E**	**689. MOON is to EARTH** as EARTH is to (A) Mars (B) moon (C) sky (D) sun (E) orbit	TURN TO PAGE 2 TOP FRAME FOR NEXT QUESTION

741. E	742. NECKLACE is to ADORNMENT as MEDAL is to (A) jewel (B) metal (C) bravery (D) bronze (E) decoration	TURN TO PAGE 2 FOR NEXT QUESTION
794. A	795. FEE is to PAY as GRAIN is to (A) eat (B) sew (C) wheat (D) sow (E) mold	TURN TO PAGE 2 FOR NEXT QUESTION
847. C	848. MONOTONY : BOREDOM :: (A) perseverence : success (B) interest : complication (C) factory : salary (D) automation : saving (E) repetition : indolence	TURN TO PAGE 2
900. B	901. MORPHINE : PAIN :: (A) symptom : illness (B) doctor : relief (C) dope : addict (D) eraser : spot (E) hope : relief	TURN TO PAGE 2
953. B	954. MODIFICATION : ADAPTED :: (A) modifier : grammatical (B) change : stable (C) replica : reproduced (D) reduction : gained	TURN TO PAGE 2 FOR NEXT QUESTION
1006. D	1007. NAIL : FINGER :: (A) apple : pie (B) foot : hand (C) tooth : comb (D) brush : hair	TURN TO PAGE 2 FOR NEXT QUESTION
1059. A	1060. TITANIC : PUNY :: (A) boat : iceberg (B) Titan : Jupiter (C) roughness : rudeness (D) melancholy : gaiety	TURN TO PAGE 2 FOR NEXT QUESTION
1112. B	1113. WET : SOAKED :: (A) bathing suit : water (B) dissonant : consonant (C) hungry : starved (D) wine : whiskey	TURN TO PAGE 2
1165. D	1166. DANCE : TANGO :: (A) fold : hands (B) review : play (C) brush : teeth (D) imagine : incident	TURN TO PAGE 2
1218. D	1219. SWIM : SWAM as BURST : (A) busted (B) bursted (C) burst (D) blurted	TURN TO PAGE 2 FOR NEXT QUESTION
1271. A	1272. MUSCLE : (A) hard (B) strong (C) desiccated (D) striated as GLANDS : ENDOCRINE	TURN TO PAGE 2 FOR NEXT QUESTION
1324. D	1325. CADENZA is to MUSIC as LOB is to (A) baseball (B) football (C) cricket (D) boxing	TURN TO PAGE 2 FOR NEXT QUESTION
1377. B	YOU HAVE JUST ANSWERED YOUR LAST PROGRAMMED QUESTION	

PART THREE

Three Sample Miller Analogies Tests

3

M.A.T. FACTS

The Miller Analogies Test is highly regarded as an instrument for the selection of graduate students. Popularly known as the MAT, it consists of 100 analogy questions embracing various disciplines including the natural and physical sciences, social sciences, mathematics, and the humanities. Although vocabulary skills are not tested as such, the college graduate who takes the test is expected to have a reasonably good verbal background.

The MAT is essentially a test of relationship recognition rather than a test of background. It is, then, a test of aptitude rather than achievement. As a high-level examination to prognosticate success in graduate studies, it assumes that the candidate has wide academic background. It follows that a great many of the questions have academic reference.

The testing period is 50 minutes and the candidate's score is simply the number of right answers. There is no penalty for incorrect answers. It is, therefore, advisable to answer every question.

THE PURPOSE OF THE SAMPLE TESTS

The three Sample Tests that follow are patterned after the actual test. They are designed to familiarize you with the types of questions which you will meet on the real test. In all fairness, we emphasize that these Sample Tests are *not* actual tests. The Miller Analogies Test is a secure test which cannot be duplicated.

THREE TIPS

The following tips are offered so that you may derive maximum benefit in the use of these three practice tests:

TIP 1—*Place yourself under strict examination conditions in taking each of the Sample Tests. Allow yourself exactly 50 minutes of working time. Tolerate no interruptions while you are taking the test. Work in a steady manner. Do not spend too much time on any one question. If a question seems too difficult, proceed to the next one. If time permits, go back to figure out the answer to the omitted question. In any case, put down an answer for the omitted question, since there is no penalty for an incorrect answer.*

TIP 2—*When the time is up, check your answers with the Answer Key which follows the Sample Test. For those questions that you got wrong, read the explanation in "Explanation of Answers" which appears right after the Answer Key.*

TIP 3—*Review the early pages of this book, xi through xvi ..."Two Important Steps to Analogy Success," "Kinds of Relationships," and "Sample Test Questions Analyzed." As you review these pages, adapt the material to the MAT question form, since there are various analogy question formats.*

Miller Analogies Test

(Sample 1)

Time: 50 minutes

Directions: From the four lettered words in parentheses, select that word which best completes the analogy which exists among the three capitalized words.

1. CROWN : ROYAL :: (A. prayer B. crucifix C. priesthood D. bible) : RELIGIOUS

2. SMALL : (A. tiny B. petite C. little D. diminutive) :: LARGE : BIG

3. WORM : BIRD :: MOUSE : (A. man B. snake C. rodent D. lion)

4. (A. artist B. description C. narration D. personality) : CHARACTERIZATION :: PICTURE : PORTRAIT

5. (A. orate B. sing C. mumble D. speak) : TALK :: SCRAWL : WRITE

6. LYNDON B. JOHNSON : (A. Henry C. Lodge B. John F. Kennedy C. Dwight D. Eisenhower D. Harry S. Truman) :: HUBERT HUMPHREY : WILLIAM MILLER

7. 15 : 6 :: 23 : (A. 8 B. 7 C. 6 D. 5)

8. STEAM : ELECTRICITY :: WATER : (A. ice B. wind C. pipe D. cord)

9. SODIUM : SALT :: OXYGEN : (A. acetylene B. carbon tetrachloride C. water D. ammonia)

10. (A. theft B. notoriety C. police D. jail) : CRIME :: CEMETERY : DEATH

11. GRASS : (A. chicken B. onion C. lettuce D. flower) :: SNOW : MILK

12. (A. second B. moment C. time D. day) : HOUR :: YARD : FOOT

13. ARGUMENT : DEBATE :: FIGHT : (A. skirmish B. contest C. challenge D. crisis)

14. PICCOLO : (A. trumpet B. trombone C. horn D. tuba) :: VIOLIN : BASS

15. HILL : MOUNTAIN :: (A. distress B. discomfort C. headache D. fear) : PAIN

16. WEALTH : TANGIBLE :: (A. price B. gold C. success D. gifts) : INTANGIBLE

17. HEMOGLOBIN : BLOOD :: COACHES : (A. train B. whip C. fuel D. fluid)

18. BREAD : CAKE :: SHIRT : (A. shoes B. tie C. pants D. coat)

19. AFFLUENT : (A. charity B. luck C. misfortune D. indifference) :: IMPOVERISHED : LAZINESS

20. INNING : BASEBALL :: (A. time B. date C. era D. year) : HISTORY

21. SHONE : DISHONEST :: LEST : (A. many B. tool C. candlestick D. lamp)

22. THROW : JAVELIN :: (A. toss B. put C. hurl D. push) : SHOT

23. MIAMI : (A. Chicago B. Jersey City C. Springfield D. Lancaster) :: PHILADELPHIA : ALBANY

24. MINERAL : MINER :: (A. agriculture B. farm C. crop D. fertilizer) : FARMER

25. (A. leopard B. mink C. sable
D. chinchilla) : LION :: TIGER :
ZEBRA

26. (A. Mars B. Vulcan C. Juno D. Apollo)
: WODIN :: LATONA : THOR

27. DREDGE : (A. channel B. barge
C. harbor D. silt) :: SCOOP : ICE
CREAM

28. LIMP : CANE :: (A. cell B. muscle
C. heat D. cold) : TISSUE

29. LIONHEARTED : RICHARD ::
KINGMAKER : (A. Warwick B. chessmen
C. Alfred D. England)

30. (A. parchment B. concrete C. cardboard
D. timber) : ADOBE :: PAPER :
PAPYRUS

31. LEGS : MORPHEUS :: (A. mouth
B. nose C. ears D. feet) : DESTINY

32. HYMN : THEIR :: CELL : (A. score
B. peal C. tree D. mile)

33. SONG : (A. sing B. melody C. swan
D. feather) :: CALL : TELEPHONE

34. (A. coal B. diamond C. pine
D. baseball) : PITCH :: SNOW : SHEET

35. COOKERY : ROOKERY :: MEAL :
(A. bird B. seal C. peal D. chess)

36. PEACH : (A. apple B. beet C. grape
D. tomato) :: CHERRY : RADISH

37. EXORBITANT : EXPENSIVE ::
PARSIMONIOUS : (A. generous B. idiotic
C. dedicated D. thrifty)

38.

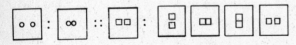

   A   B   C   D

39. LEAF : (A. freedom B. indifference
C. thought D. wall) :: BRIDGE :
UMBRELLA

40. (A. earth B. Venus C. sputnik D. berry)
: PLANET :: CANAL : RIVER

41. PIRAEUS : OSTIA :: (A. Athens B.
Florence C. Milan D. Crete) : ROME

42. (A. psychology B. philology C. philosophy
D. philately) : PHRENOLOGY ::
ASTRONOMY : ASTROLOGY

43. FORETOKEN : (A. portend B. augur
C. bode D. presage) :: DIVINE :
PREDICT

44. STUDENT : DEW :: SIEVE : (A. receive
B. relieve C. reprieve D. give)

45. LINEAGE : GENEALOGY :: (A. science
B. events C. economics D. chronology) :
HISTORY

46. ROMAN : (A. Caesar B. Rembrandt
C. gladiator D. Van Dyke) :: NOSE :
BEARD

47. BEND : ELBOW :: (A. strip B. dissect
C. skin D. divide) : CAT

48. (A. walking B. foot C. step D. instep) :
TOES :: NIB : RESERVOIR

49. 19 : 23 :: (A. 7 B. 11 C. 13 D. 17) :
13

50. HIPS : CHURCH DOOR :: ABYSS :
(A. truth B. bond C. speck D. ocean)

51. (A. Laos B. Indonesia C. Afghanistan
D. Japan) : INDIA :: NEVADA :
COLORADO

52. CONCISE : (A. refined B. expanded
C. precise D. blunt) :: REMOVE :
OBLITERATE

53. SAGACIOUS : OBTUSE :: GRAVE :
(A. tomb B. somber C. jocular
D. severe)

54. AHOY : SAILOR :: (A. fore B. hail
C. timber D. putter) : GOLFER

55. JACKET : (A. lapel B. button C. vest
D. collar) :: PANTS : CUFF

56. COMA : HOTEL :: MORPHINE :
(A. frog   B. blanket   C. horse   D. ship)

57. (A. Athena   B. Ceres   C. Artemis
D. Aphrodite) : ZEUS :: EVE : ADAM

58. SERAPHIC : (A. Napoleonic
B. Mephistophelian   C. Alexandrine
D. euphoric) :: ALACRITY : LANGUOR

59. TIGER : SERGEANT :: (A. elm   B. oak
C. army   D. general) : MAJOR

60. (A. precarious   B. deleterious   C. deterred
D. immortal) : DEADLY ::
CELEBRATED : LIONIZED

61. MANET : REMBRANDT :: (A. Picasso
B. Dali   C. Pollack   D. Cezanne) : VAN
GOGH

62. (A. glove   B. stocking   C. weakness
D. mitt) : GAUNTLET :: HAT :
HELMET

63. STIRRUP : COCHLEA :: BRIM :
(A. hat   B. derby   C. crown   D. head)

64. (A. rococo   B. severe   C. Etruscan
D. stylish) : ORNAMENTED :: SOGGY
: MOIST

65. SCINTILLA : (A. odor   B. sparkle
C. heap   D. microbe) :: SIBERIA :
PACIFIC

66. NEW YORK : RHODES :: LIBERTY :
(A. Apollo   B. scholar   C. tyranny
D. freedom)

67. RUBY : TOMATO :: (A. rose
B. assassin   C. peach   D. shamrock) :
EMERALD

68. WATER : (A. mercury   B. steam
C. copper   D. chemical) :: ICE : IRON

69. (A. royal   B. kingly   C. regal   D. princely)
: LAGER :: TIME : EMIT

70. CLAY : RADIATOR :: POTATO :
(A. peak   B. watch   C. daisy   D. sun)

71. ARKANSAS : FLORIDA :: NEW
MEXICO : (A. Tennessee   B. Ohio
C. California   D. Illinois) .

72. SIN : ATONE :: (A. deed   B. error
C. insult   D. argument) : APOLOGIZE

73. (A. solo   B. duet   C. trio   D. quartet) :
QUINTET :: PRIZEFIGHT :
BASKETBALL

74. PIPE : POT :: (A. scrub   B. ream
C. scourge   D. drain) : SCOUR

75. (A. erosion   B. expansion   C. contraction
D. fluidity) : WATER :: WRINKLES :
AGE

76. (A. Jupiter   B. Hippocrates   C. Petrarch
D. Shakespeare) : ALFRED ::
CADUCEUS : SCEPTER

77. RADAR : DEPT. :: (A. telephone
B. radio   C. laser   D. telegraph) : ACCT.

78. EPISTEMOLOGY : (A. letters
B. weapons   C. knowledge   D. roots) ::
PALEONTOLOGY : FOSSILS

79. (A. stick   B. foundry   C. corps   D. fife) :
DRUM :: FLINT : STEEL

80. TURN : (A. pass   B. decline   C. avoid
D. skip) :: EYE : BLINK

81. PLATO : (A. Socrates   B. Sophocles
C. Aristophanes   D. Aristotle) :: FREUD :
JUNG

82. (A. law   B. book   C. band   D. wagon) :
WAINWRIGHT :: DICTIONARY :
LEXICOGRAPHER

83. LOOSE : ROUT :: (A. tomb   B. stock
C. mouth   D. ridge) : MOUSE

84. CONCERT : (A. andante   B. a cappella
C. opera   D. music) :: PERFORMANCE :
PANTOMIME

85. (A. uniform   B. commander   C. platoon
D. sentry) : DOG :: GARRISON :
FLOCK

86. PORTUGAL : IBERIA :: TOOTH :
(A. dentist   B. cavity   C. nail   D. comb)

87. (A. shoe   B. saddle   C. withers   D. bridle)
: HORSE :: COLLAR : DOG

88. BINDING : (A. book   B. library   C. page
    D. leather) :: SOLE : LACE

89. (A. hand   B. brow   C. eye   D. leg) :
    KNIT :: DICTATION : TAKE

90. INTAGLIO : (A. cameo   B. caviar
    C. Machiavellian   D. harem) :: CONCAVE
    : CONVEX

91. ORCHESTRA : (A. mezzanine   B. stage
    C. proscenium   D. second balcony) ::
    ABDOMEN : THORAX

92. AMPLITUDE : SURFEIT :: (A. Jacobean
    B. strong   C. onerous   D. pleasant) :
    HERCULEAN

93. LOYALTY : FRIEND :: (A. allegiance
    B. love   C. respect   D. nation) : FLAG

94. (A. fjord   B. ford   C. Ford   D. afford) :
    STREAM :: BRIDGE : RIVER

95. VERDI : (A. Italian   B. Fidelio
    C. violinist   D. Rigoletto) :: CHOPIN :
    PARSIFAL

96. SUBSTITUTE : TEAM ::
    UNDERSTUDY : (A. crew
    B. congregation   C. actor   D. cast)

97. PORT : (A. vintage   B. harbor
    C. starboard   D. left) :: HEADLIGHTS :
    TRUNK

98. MIAMI BEACH : LAS VEGAS ::
    CANNES : (A. Provincetown   B. Asbury
    Park   C. Sun Valley   D. Atlantic City)

99. (A. fish   B. breath   C. Jill   D. quart) :
    GILL :: OCTAVE : MONOTHEISM

100. ROOSTER : (A. crow   B. coop   C. fox
     D. owl) :: EFFERVESCENT : EFFETE

END OF MILLER ANALOGIES TEST (SAMPLE 1)

Answer Sheet

(Answer bubble grid, questions 1–100, each with options a b c d e)

Correct Answers For The Foregoing Questions

(Please make every effort to answer the questions on your own before looking at these answers. You'll make faster progress by following this rule.)

1. B	15. B	27. D	39. D	51. C	63. C	75. A	87. D
2. C	16. C	28. D	40. C	52. D	64. A	76. B	88. C
3. B	17. A	29. A	41. A	53. C	65. D	77. C	89. B
4. B	18. B	30. B	42. A	54. A	66. A	78. C	90. A
5. C	19. B	31. D	43. A	55. A	67. D	79. D	91. A
6. A	20. C	32. B	44. D	56. B	68. A	80. D	92. C
7. D	21. C	33. C	45. D	57. A	69. C	81. D	93. A
8. B	22. B	34. A	46. D	58. B	70. D	82. D	94. B
9. C	23. C	35. A	47. C	59. B	71. C	83. A	95. B
10. D	24. C	36. B	48. D	60. B	72. C	84. B	96. D
11. C	25. B	37. D	49. B	61. D	73. A	85. D	97. C
12. D	26. C	38. B	50. D	62. A	74. B	86. D	98. C
13. B							99. D
14. D							100. D

EXPLANATION OF ANSWERS FOR SAMPLE TEST 1

1. **(B)** A crown (when worn) indicates a royal state; a crucifix (when worn) indicates a religious attachment. Note that a bible also indicates a religious attachment, but the bible is not worn.

2. **(C)** A general synonym for small is little; tiny, petite, and diminutive have special connotations. The word big is a special synonym for large.

3. **(B)** Birds like to eat worms; snakes like to eat mice.

4. **(B)** A characterization is a kind of description—usually a description of a person; a portrait is a kind of picture—usually a picture of a person.

5. **(C)** To mumble is to talk carelessly, thus making it difficult to be understood; to scrawl is to write carelessly so that it is difficult to be understood.

6. **(A)** Johnson was a successful vice-presidential candidate at the time that Lodge was an unsuccessful vice-presidential candidate; Humphrey was successful—Miller was defeated—also, for the vice-presidential office.

7. **(D)** $1 + 5 = 6$; $2 + 3 = 5$

8. **(B)** Steam and water are visible; electricity and wind are invisible.

9. **(C)** Sodium is one of the elements that make up salt; oxygen is one of the elements that make up water.

10. **(D)** Crime usually lands the person in jail; death usually lands the person in a cemetery.

11. **(C)** Snow and milk are white; grass and lettuce are green.

12. **(D)** A foot is a unit measure of a yard; an hour is a unit measure of a day.

13. **(B)** An argument has considerable emotional implication—a debate has little such implication; a fight has considerable emotional implication—a contest has little such implication.

14. **(D)** A piccolo is a wind instrument pitched an octave higher than an ordinary flute, whereas a tuba is a much larger and lower-pitched wind instrument; a violin, in comparison with a bass, is smaller and higher-pitched.

15. **(B)** A hill is a smaller version of a mountain; discomfort is a smaller version of pain. Note that a headache is a specific type of pain or discomfort.

16. **(C)** Wealth is measured by tangible units (dollars, property, etc.); success cannot be measured by tangible units.

17. **(A)** Hemoglobin is part of blood; coaches constitute part of a train.

18. **(B)** Cake is a luxury—bread is a necessity; a tie is a luxury—a shirt is a necessity.

19. **(B)** Luck is one possible factor contributory to making one affluent; laziness is one possible factor contributory to making a person impoverished.

20. **(C)** An accepted division of a baseball game is an inning; phases of history are eras.

21. **(C)** Shone is an interior part of the word dishonest; lest is an interior part of the word candlestick.

22. **(B)** A javelin throw and a shot put are both field contests.

23. **(C)** Miami and Philadelphia are chief cities; Springfield and Albany are state capitals.

24. **(C)** A miner's objective is getting the mineral; a farmer's objective is harvesting the crop.

25. **(B)** The mink and lion are brown; the tiger and zebra are striped.

26. **(C)** Juno is a goddess—Wodin is a god; Latona is a goddess—Thor is a god.

27. **(D)** One dredges silt and scoops ice cream.

28. **(D)** A person with a limp is likely to use a cane; a person with a cold is likely to use a tissue.

29. **(A)** Richard was known as the Lionhearted —Warwick as the Kingmaker.

30. **(B)** Concrete is a modern building material —adobe is little used today; paper, as a writing material, has replaced papyrus.

31. **(D)** We speak of being in the arms (antonym = legs) of Morpheus and in the hands (antonym = feet) of Destiny.

32. **(B)** Each of the following has a homophone: Hymn (him); their (there); cell (sell); peal (peel)

33. **(C)** We speak of a swan song and a telephone call.

34. **(A)** As black (coal) as pitch—as white (snow) as a sheet.

35. **(A)** A cookery is where a meal is made; a rookery is where a bird is produced.

36. **(B)** A peach grows above the ground—a beet below; a cherry grows above the ground —a radish below.

37. **(D)** Exorbitant means unreasonably expensive; parsimonious means unreasonably thrifty.

38. **(B)** In the second square, the circles are moved together and the circle on the right is darkened; in the B choice, the squares are moved together and the right-hand square is darkened.

39. **(D)** A leaf and a wall are concrete nouns; so are a bridge and an umbrella.

40. **(C)** Man-made sputnik was put into orbit— a planet is in orbit naturally; a canal is a man-made river.

41. **(A)** Piraeus is a port city near Athens; Ostia was a port city near Rome.

42. **(A)** Psychology is an accepted science dealing with the brain—phrenology, dealing with head formation, is not an accepted science; astronomy is an accepted science dealing with the heavens—astrology, dealing with the stars, is not an accepted science.

43. **(A)** Only things foretoken and portend; only persons divine and predict.

44. **(D)** Student has the same vowel sound as dew; sieve has the same vowel sound as give.

45. **(D)** Lineage is a "time tree" with family branches—all of this constitutes the study of genealogy; chronology is an order of events according to time—this is what history consists of.

46. **(D)** We speak of a Roman nose and a Van Dyke beard.

47. **(C)** You bend an elbow and skin a cat.

48. **(D)** The instep and toes are parts of the foot; the nib and reservoir are parts of the pen.

49. **(B)** A prime number is one which has no factors which yield quotients (other than one or that prime number). 19 is the highest prime number lower than 23. Similarly, 11 is the highest prime number lower than 13.

50. **(D)** Hips and a church door have the measure quality of width; an abyss and an ocean have the measure quality of depth.

51. **(C)** Afghanistan and India are countries separated by another country (Pakistan); Nevada and Colorado are states separated by another state (Utah).

52. **(D)** A concise person is to the point—a blunt person is rudely to the point; obliterate is to remove completely or by destruction.

53. **(C)** Sagacious and obtuse are antonyms—so are grave and jocular.

54. **(A)** Ahoy is a sailor cry; fore is a golfer cry.

55. **(A)** A lapel is a folded over part of a jacket; a cuff is a folded over part of pants.

56. **(B)** All of the following are associated with sleep: coma, hotel, morphine, blanket.

57. **(A)** Athena is said to have sprung from the head of Zeus—Eve from the rib of Adam.

58. **(B)** Seraphic and mephistophelian are antonyms—so are alacrity and languor.

59. **(B)** Stripes (tiger) are emblematic of the rank of sergeant; an oak leaf is emblematic of the rank of major.

60. **(B)** Something that is very deleterious may prove deadly; a person who is much celebrated may be lionized.

61. **(D)** Manet and Cezanne were French painters; Rembrandt and Van Gogh were Dutch painters.

62. **(A)** A glove is a peace-time hand covering—a gauntlet was used for hand protection in combat; a hat is a peace-time head covering—a helmet is used in time of war.

63. **(C)** The stirrup and cochlea are parts of the ear; the brim and crown are parts of a hat.

64. **(A)** Rococo is excessively ornate; soggy is heavily moist.

65. **(D)** A scintilla and a microbe are small; Siberia and the Pacific are vast.

66. **(A)** The statue of Liberty is set at the entrance to the harbor of New York; a statue of Apollo was set at the entrance to the harbor of ancient Rhodes.

67. **(D)** A ruby and a tomato are red; a shamrock and an emerald are green.

68. **(A)** Water and mercury flow as liquids; ice and iron, as solids, do not flow.

69. **(C)** Regal spelled backwards is lager; time spelled backwards is emit.

70. **(D)** Heat (a radiator gives heat) is used to bake clay; heat (the sun gives heat) is used to bake a potato.

71. **(C)** Arkansas and New Mexico are interior states; Florida and California are peninsular states.

72. **(C)** One atones to make up for a sin; one apologizes to make up for an insult.

73. **(A)** A prizefight has one contestant on each side; a basketball game has five contestants on each side.

74. **(B)** You ream a pipe and you scour a pot.

75. **(A)** Water causes erosion; age causes wrinkles.

76. **(B)** A caduceus is a symbol of medicine—Hippocrates was a physician; a scepter is a symbol of kingship—Alfred was a king.

77. **(C)** Radar and laser are acronyms; dept. and acct. are abbreviations.

78. **(C)** Epistemology is concerned with knowledge; paleontology is concerned with fossils.

79. **(D)** A pipe is used with a drum to make up a corps; flint is used with steel to produce fire.

80. **(D)** You skip a turn and blink an eye.

81. **(D)** Aristotle was a follower of Plato; Jung was a follower of Freud.

82. **(D)** A lexicographer composes a dictionary; a wainwright makes a wheel.

83. **(A)** Loose and tomb have the same vowel sounds; rout and mouse have the same vowel sounds.

84. **(B)** A concert in which there is singing without musical accompaniment is a capella; a dramatic performance in which there is no dialogue is a pantomime.

85. **(D)** A sentry guards a garrison—a dog guards a flock.

86. **(D)** Portugal is part of the peninsula of Iberia; a tooth is part of a comb.

87. **(D)** When the rider pulls at the reins of the bridle, the horse is restrained; the leash attached to the collar holds back the dog.

88. **(C)** The binding and the page are parts of a book; the sole and the lace are parts of a shoe.

89. **(B)** You knit a brow and you take dictation.

90. **(A)** Intaglio is incised carving—a cameo is something carved in relief; concave means curving inward—convex means curving outward.

91. **(A)** The mezzanine is located directly above the orchestra; the thorax is situated directly above the abdomen.

92. **(C)** When there is considerable amplitude, there is a surfeit; when a task is very onerous, it is herculean.

93. **(A)** One pledges loyalty to a friend and allegiance to a flag.

94. **(B)** One crosses a stream by fording it; one crosses a river by bridging it.

95. **(B)** Verdi did not compose *Fidelio;* Chopin did not compose *Parsifal.*

96. **(D)** A substitute is used to replace someone on a team; an understudy is used to replace someone in a cast.

97. **(C)** The port side and the starboard side are opposite sides of a ship; the headlights and trunk are at extreme ends of an automobile.

98. **(C)** Miami Beach and Las Vegas are famous resorts—the first with a beach, the second without a beach; Cannes and Sun Valley are famous resorts—the first with a beach, the second without a beach.

99. **(D)** There are eight gills in one quart; an octave is a group of eight—monotheism is the belief in one god.

100. **(D)** A rooster crows in the morning—an owl, conversely, is active at night; effervescent means exuberant—effete, on the other hand, means lacking vigor.

ANSWER SHEET FOR SAMPLE MAT

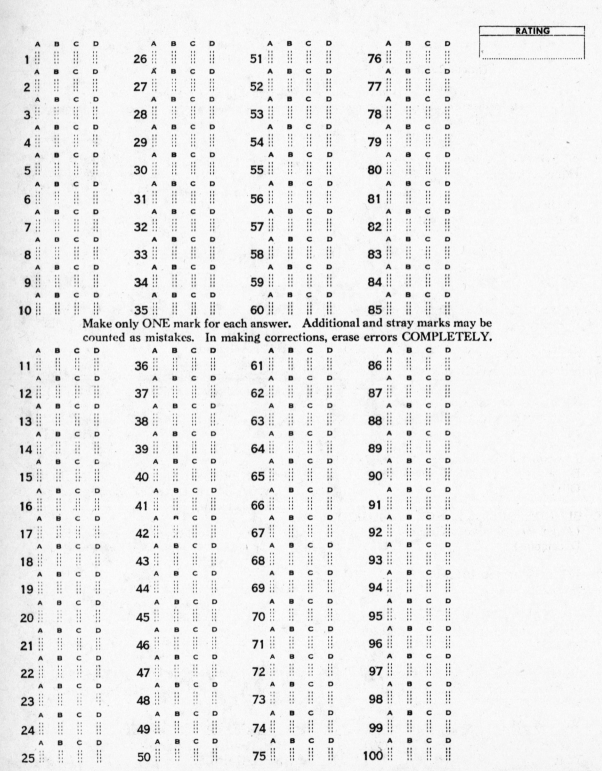

Make only ONE mark for each answer. Additional and stray marks may be counted as mistakes. In making corrections, erase errors COMPLETELY.

Miller Analogies Test

(Sample 2)

Time: 50 minutes

Directions: From the four lettered words in parentheses, select that word which best completes the analogy which exists among the three capitalized words.

1. NEEDLE : (A. thread   B. pen   C. pole   D. hole) :: PENCIL : ARROW

2. CLUE : DETECTIVE :: (A. stethoscope   B. disease   C. symptom   D. medicine) : DOCTOR

3. (A. egg   B. planet   C. lemon   D. record) : ORANGE :: DIME : WHEEL

4. NEWSPRINT : (A. paper   B. linotype   C. newsstand   D. tree) :: STEEL : ORE

5. GOLF : RACING :: GREEN : (A. grass   B. lawn   C. turf   D. yellow)

6. SONAR : (A. airplane   B. electronics   C. submarine   D. detection) :: RADAR : STORM

7. (A. thunder   B. lightning   C. melodious   D. cloudy) : LOUD :: CONCERT : ONCE

8. BLUNDERBUSS : LANCE :: MUSKET : (A. missile   B. pistol   C. bomb   D. catapult)

9. 121 : 12 :: (A. 101   B. 141   C. 100   D. 125) : 11

10. CLAWING : (A. scratching   B. devouring   C. crippling   D. pawing) :: VIOLENT : BRASH

11. (A. Tannhauser   B. opera   C. rose   D. Pinafore) : WAGNER :: CARMEN : MOZART

12. STARTLED : (A. interested   B. astounded   C. expected   D. unknown) :: WORK : TOIL

13. BRAGGADOCIO : RETICENCE :: MISER : (A. profligacy   B. obesity   C. obloquy   D. falsity)

14. (A. mined   B. minor   C. miner   D. canvas) : DENIM :: GULP : PLUG

15. SANDHURST : ENGLAND :: (A. Harvard   B. Pittsburgh   C. West Point   D. Norwalk) : UNITED STATES

16. BURGUNDY : VINTNER :: (A. eggs   B. drugs   C. candles   D. ropes) : CHANDLER

17. (A. tactics   B. strategy   C. maneuvers   D. regiment) : ARMY :: PUPIL : EYE

18. PARIS : (A. France   B. London   C. Achilles   D. garter) :: ACHILLES : HECTOR

19. GENEROUS : LAVISH :: TIMOROUS : (A. timid   B. craven   C. courageous   D. foolhardy)

20. MECCA : MOSLEM :: BENARES : (A. Islam   B. India   C. Hindu   D. Granges)

21. BRANCH : DESK :: (A. pole   B. paint   C. street   D. flag) : FLOOR

22. (A. barber   B. bristle   C. comb   D. stroke) : BRUSH :: CRUISER : FLEET

23. HUDSON : BUICK :: PACKARD : (A. Stutz   B. Locomobile   C. Maxwell   D. Oldsmobile)

24. MACBETH : TEMPEST :: (A. assassin   B. Pontiac   C. gravity   D. storm) : FICKLENESS

25. (A. Galen B. oath C. classic D. Pericles) : HIPPOCRATES :: SCHWEITZER : SALK

26. TAME : (A. testament B. will C. gospel D. wild) :: ROLL : CONTROLLER

27. RECEIVE : DIARRHEA :: PENNICILIN : (A. figure B. classification C. batallion D. geometry)

28. (A. lunch B. meal C. breakfast D. brunch) : SUPPER :: SMOG : HAZE

29. THREE : FIVE :: (A. Jefferson B. memorial C. Monticello D. Lincoln) : MONROE

30.

A   B   C   D

31. SCALE : RING :: PAT : (A. boil B. barn C. piano D. grass)

32. (A. happiness B. chest C. discouragement D. female) : HOPE :: DARKNESS : SUNRISE

33. BLUE : ORANGE :: (A. indigo B. yellow C. purple D. red) : GREEN

34. CHEETAH : SPEED :: (A. blade B. cleavage S. alertness D. incision) : KEENNESS

35. (A. hock B. jockey C. stable D. hand) : HORSE :: TONGUE : BELL

36. TENANT : ANT :: SYLLOGISM : (A. logic B. log C. deduction D. induction)

37. (A. Nantucket B. Puerto Rico C. Hawaii D. Long Island) : UNITED STATES :: TASMANIA : AUSTRALIA

38. ANCHISES : (A. Troilus B. Achilles C. Ajax D. Aeneas) :: PRIAM : HECTOR

39. SELDOM : FREQUENTLY :: ETERNALLY : (A. never B. occasionally irregularly D. now and then)

40. DEVIL : LIVED :: GOLF : (A. club B. polo C. whip D. flog)

41. MAP : (A. explorer B. geography C. legend D. atlas) :: TEXT : FOOTNOTE

42. (A. clock B. watch C. time D. hour) : TELL :: GUM : CHEW

43. CALENDAR : CALENDER :: LEAF : (A. lief B. leif C. leef D. leafe)

44. COOPER : BARREL :: (A. lithographer B. cartographer C. photographer D. biographer) : MAP

45. PUPA : (A. tadpole B. larva C. cocoon D. bumblebee) :: FETUS : CHILD

46. IRON : CORRUGATION :: (A. brow B. wart C. toad D. age) : WRINKLE

47. SILENCE : (A. muffle B. cry C. hear D. speak) :: LIE : FIB

48. (A. Crete B. Malta C. Sicily D. Corsica) : SARDINIA :: BOLIVIA : ARGENTINA

49. EVIL : EXORCISE :: BREAD : (A. carve B. break C. slit D. shred)

50. OR : (A. sable B. gules C. argent D. vert) :: YOLK : ALBUMEN

51. (A. humid B. speedy C. piquant D. moist) : VAPID :: OBDURATE : COMPASSIONATE

52. CUCUMBER : WATERMELON :: CANTALOUPE : (A. squash B. radish C. cherry D. plum)

53. (A. head B. nose C. ear D. limb) : MAN :: STRING : VIOLIN

54. ILLNESS : (A. debility B. hospital C. doctor D. panacea) :: VIBRATION : SOUND

55. GETTYSBURG : VICKSBURG :: LEXINGTON : (A. Trenton B. Pittsburgh C. Eisenhower D. Waterloo)

56. (A. gain B. reward C. loot D. profit) :
ROBBERY :: REVENGE : VENDETTA

57. UNCONSCIOUS : FREUD ::
(A. manipulation B. illness C. sex
D. stimulation) : OSTEOPATHY

58. CLAUSTROPHOBIA : CLOSETS ::
AGORAPHOBIA : (A. ships B. sheep
C. plants D. plains)

59. (A. silence B. cheese C. cat D. trap) :
MOUSE :: GRACE : GAZELLE

60. (A. sympathy B. encouragement
C. blasphemy D. solidity) : FRACAS ::
APHRODITE : MARS

61. CHEESE : ROSE :: GASOLINE :
(A. fence B. sulphur C. sky D. glass)

62. WALK : (A. shoe B. ride C. club
D. king) :: REEF : FIND

63. (A. cathedral B. altar C. steeple
D. nave) : CHURCH :: MINARET :
MOSQUE

64. CROESUS : (A. boat B. wealth
C. pleats D. loyalty) :: ODYSSEUS :
CRAFT

65. LUCERNE : MICHIGAN :: GENEVA :
(A. watch B. conference C. Okeechobee
D. Switzerland)

66. (A. scourge B. game C. concert D. run)
: SCORE :: PLAY : SCRIPT

67. HERRING : (A. salt B. sea C. egg
D. ham) :: CIGARETTE : VOLCANO

68. DDT : INSECT :: (A. castle B. fire
C. knight D. maiden) : DRAGON

69. (A. pear B. plywood C. maple D. brass)
: WOOD :: NECTARINE : PEACH

70. PARTRIDGE : WASP :: (A. quail
B. sting C. birds D. covey) : NEST

71. LAPIDARY : (A. ruby B. wood C. lick
D. food) :: SCULPTOR : ALABASTER

72. WOOF : FILE :: WARP : (A. grade
B. rank C. parade D. twist)

73. SMILE : (A. rile B. style C. while
D. tile) :: SCHEMES : DREAMS

74. FORSOOK : DRANK :: FROZEN :
(A. swum B. wrote C. sang D. chose)

75. SANDAL : BOOT :: (A. hammer
B. hatchet C. shoemaker D. blade) : AX

76. HORSE : (A. man B. goat C. archer
D. bull) :: CENTAUR : SATYR

77. (A. anode B. bird C. purchase
D. battery) : CELL :: FEATHER :
SHAFT

78. GNAT : (A. kimono B. spagetti
C. embarrassment D. perseverance) ::
ACCOMMODATION : ECSTACY

79. NOVEMBER : APRIL :: (A. May
B. June C. July D. August) :
SEPTEMBER

80. ENTRY : FINEST :: INITIATIVE :
(A. halibut B. jewelry C. binder
D. esteem)

81. (A. wasteful B. wandering C. stationary
D. frugal) : PRODIGAL ::
DISINTERESTED : PARTIAL

82. EIFFEL : PISA :: (A. submarine
B. schooner C. jet plane D. paddle) :
ROWBOAT

83. (A. pine B. cedar C. ash D. willow) :
OAK :: MOURNFUL : STURDY

84. ADVISE : EXHORT :: (A. force
B. tempt C. prohibit D. prevent) :
ENTICE

85. STEEL : WELD :: LIPS : (A. frown
B. purse C. fold D. smirk)

86. TESTIMONY : (A. confession B. judge
C. witness D. trial) :: BIOGRAPHY :
AUTOBIOGRAPHY

87. (A. Hinduism B. Mohammedanism
C. Protestantism D. Catholicism) :
BUDDHISM :: ZOROASTRIANISM :
CONFUCIANISM

88. LAMB : DEER :: (A. rabbit   B. peacock
C. snake   D. pig) : LION

89. BUILDING : (A. contractor   B. city
C. foundation   D. blueprint) :: CAT :
FUR

90. (A. distance   B. program   C. station
D. tube) : TELEVISION :: LEADER :
ANARCHY

91. TATOO : VESPERS :: (A. painting
B. needle   C. revelry   D. reveille) :
MATINS

92. PROSTRATE : (A. dazzling   B. stealing
C. yielding   D. dreaming) :: SUPINE :
SLEEPING

93. WHALE : TROUT :: HARPOON :
(A. fly   B. worm   C. javelin   D. bait)

94. SKIING : (A. snowshoe   B. skate

C. winter   D. hockey) :: SNOW : ICE

95. (A. bone   B. biology   C. anatomy
D. laboratory) : SKELETON :: WOOD :
TREE

96. TINE : FORK :: (A. car   B. gearshift
C. flange   D. wheelwright) : WHEEL

97. (A. tie   B. appearance   C. tuxedo
D. decoration) : ATTIRE :: WIT :
COMMUNICATION

98. SPARE : (A. strike   B. allowance   C. spire
D. tire) :: RUN : HOMERUN

99. (A. grind   B. thresh   C. harvest   D. grow)
: WHEAT :: DISTILL : WATER

100. SYBARITE : (A. luxury   B. abstemiousness
C. intelligence   D. sincerity) :: SPARTAN
: GARRULITY

END OF MILLER ANALOGIES TEST (SAMPLE 2)

Answer Sheet

	a	b	c	d	e
1					
5					
9					
13					
17					
21					
25					
29					
33					
37					
41					
45					
49					
53					
57					
61					
65					
69					
73					
77					
81					
85					
89					
93					
97					

	a	b	c	d	e
2					
6					
10					
14					
18					
22					
26					
30					
34					
38					
42					
46					
50					
54					
58					
62					
66					
70					
74					
78					
82					
86					
90					
94					
98					

	a	b	c	d	e
3					
7					
11					
15					
19					
23					
27					
31					
35					
39					
43					
47					
51					
55					
59					
63					
67					
71					
75					
79					
83					
87					
91					
95					
99					

	a	b	c	d	e
4					
8					
12					
16					
20					
24					
28					
32					
36					
40					
44					
48					
52					
56					
60					
64					
68					
72					
76					
80					
84					
88					
92					
96					
100					

Correct Answers For The Foregoing Questions

(Please make every effort to answer the questions on your own before look-
ing at these answers. You'll make faster progress by following this rule.)

1. B	15. C	27. C	39. A	51. C	63. C	75. B	87. B
2. C	16. C	28. D	40. D	52. A	64. B	76. B	88. B
3. B	17. D	29. A	41. C	53. D	65. C	77. D	89. C
4. D	18. C	30. C	42. C	54. A	66. C	78. B	90. A
5. C	19. B	31. A	43. A	55. A	67. D	79. B	91. D
6. C	20. C	32. C	44. B	56. C	68. D	80. B	92. C
7. D	21. A	33. D	45. D	57. A	69. B	81. D	93. A
8. D	22. B	34. A	46. A	58. D	70. D	82. B	94. D
9. C	23. D	35. A	47. A	59. A	71. A	83. D	95. A
10. A	24. C	36. B	48. D	60. A	72. B	84. B	96. C
11. D	25. A	37. C	49. B	61. B	73. B	85. B	97. D
12. B	26. A	38. D	50. C	62. D	74. A	86. A	98. A
13. A							99. B
14. A							100. B

EXPLANATION OF ANSWERS FOR MAT SAMPLE TEST 2

1. **(B)** All of the following have points: a needle, a pen, a pencil, an arrow.

2. **(C)** A detective considers a clue as a springboard to the solution of a crime; a doctor studies a symptom as a springboard to curing a disease.

3. **(B)** A planet and an orange are spherical; a dime and a wheel are cylindrical.

4. **(D)** Newsprint is made from pulp which, in turn, comes from a tree; steel is made from iron which, in turn, comes from ore.

5. **(C)** Golf is a sport engaged in on the green; racing is engaged in on the turf.

6. **(C)** Sonar is a device that uses underwater sound waves to detect a submarine; radar is a device that may locate a storm.

7. **(D)** The second, third, fourth, and fifth letters of cloudy and concert are *loud* and *once* respectively.

8. **(D)** A blunderbuss and a lance are out-of-use weapons; so are a musket and a catapult.

9. **(C)** $11^2 = 121 \ldots 11 + 1 = 12;$
$10^2 = 100 \ldots 10 + 1 = 11$

10. **(A)** Clawing is an extreme degree of scratching; violence is an extreme degree of brashness.

11. **(D)** Wagner did not compose *Pinafore;* Mozart did not compose *Carmen.*

12. **(B)** *Startled* is a milder state than *astounded; work* is a milder activity than *toil.*

13. **(A)** A braggadocio certainly does not practice reticence; a miser certainly is not guilty of profligacy.

14. **(A)** *Mined* spelled backwards is *denim; plug* spelled backwards is *gulp.*

15. **(C)** Sandhurst is the English college which trains future military officers; West Point has the same function in the United States.

16. **(C)** A vintner makes wines including burgundy; a chandler makes candles.

17. **(D)** A regiment is part of an army; a pupil is part of an eye.

18. **(C)** In Homer's *Iliad,* Paris slew Achilles—Achilles had slain Hector previously.

19. **(B)** A person who is extremely generous is lavish; a person who is extremely timid is craven.

20. **(C)** Mecca is the sacred city of the Moslems; Benares is the sacred city of the Hindus.

21. **(A)** A branch consists of wood—a desk is often made of wood; a pole and a floor are often made of wood.

22. **(B)** A bristle is part of a brush—a cruiser is part of a fleet.

23. **(D)** A Hudson is an "extinct" car—a Buick is current; a Packard is "extinct"—an Oldsmobile is current.

24. **(C)** *Macbeth* is a tragedy—*The Tempest* is a comedy; gravity means seriousness—fickleness means capriciousness.

25. **(A)** Galen, Hippocrates, Schweitzer, and Salk are physicians.

26. **(A)** The letters of the word *tame* are contained in the word *testament;* the letters of the word *roll* are contained in the word *controller.*

27. **(C)** *Receive* and *diarrhea* are spelled correctly; *pennicilin* and *batallion* are spelled incorrectly.

28. **(D)** Brunch is a combination of two meals (breakfast and lunch)—supper is one meal; smog is a combination of two atmospheric conditions (smoke and fog)—haze is one condition.

29. **(A)** Jefferson was the third president—Monroe, the fifth.

30. **(C)** A vertical line has the same relationship to a horizontal line that a rectangle standing on its end has to a rectangle lying on its side.

31. **(A)** *Scale* is a word with two different meanings—so are the words *ring, pat,* and *boil.* These are called homographs.

32. **(C)** Discouragment is an antonym of encouragement—the latter brings hope; darkness is an antonym of light—the latter is associated with sunrise.

33. **(D)** Blue and orange are complementary colors; so are red and green.

34. **(A)** A cheetah is known for its speed; a blade is proverbial for its keenness.

35. **(A)** A hock is part of a horse; a tongue is part of a bell.

36. **(B)** *Ant* is part of the word *tenant; log* is part of the word *syllogism.*

37. **(C)** Tasmania is an island state of Australia; Hawaii is an island state of the United States.

38. **(D)** Anchises was the father of Aeneas; Priam was the father of Hector.

39. **(A)** *Seldom* is an antonym of *frequently; eternally* is an antonym of *never.*

40. **(D)** *Devil* is *lived* spelled backwards; *golf* is *flog* spelled backwards.

41. **(C)** The legend explains the contents of a map; a footnote is an explanatory reference to the text.

42. **(C)** You tell time and you chew gum.

43. **(A)** *Calendar, calender, leaf,* and *lief* are correctly spelled words.

44. **(B)** A cooper makes barrels—a cartographer makes maps.

45. **(D)** The pupa is the last stage before the emergence of the bumblebee; the fetus is the last stage before the emergence of the child.

46. **(A)** Corrugated iron and a wrinkled brow have a similar appearance.

47. **(A)** When you muffle something, you are not quite silencing it; when you fib, you are just mildly lying.

48. **(D)** Corsica is an island located directly north of the island of Sardinia; Bolivia is a country directly north of Argentina.

49. **(B)** You exorcise evil; you break bread.

50. **(C)** Or is the color yellow—argent is white; the yolk is yellow—the albumen is the white of an egg.

51. **(C)** Piquant and vapid are antonyms; so are obdurate and compassionate.

52. **(A)** All four have seeds: cucumber, watermelon, cantaloupe, squash.

53. **(D)** A man has four limbs; a violin has four strings.

54. **(A)** Illness causes debility; vibration causes sound.

55. **(A)** Gettysburg and Vicksburg were battles fought in the same war (Civil War); Lexington and Trenton were battles fought in the same war (Revolutionary War).

56. **(C)** Revenge is the object of a vendetta; loot is the object of a robbery.

57. **(A)** Followers of Freud seek to alleviate mental disorders by analysis of the unconscious; those who practice osteopathy attempt to heal by manipulation of the affected parts.

58. **(D)** A person suffering from claustrophobia would fear closets; a person suffering from agoraphobia would fear plains.

59. **(A)** These are common expressions: as quiet as a mouse—as graceful as a gazelle.

60. **(A)** Aphrodite, as the goddess of love, would encourage sympathy; Mars, as the god of War, would encourage a fracas.

61. **(B)** Cheese, a rose, gasoline, and sulphur are all associated with odors.

62. **(D)** The last letter of walk is the first letter of king; the last letter of reef is the first letter of find.

63. **(C)** A steeple rises above a church; a minaret is a high slender tower rising above a mosque.

64. **(B)** Croesus was known for his wealth—Odysseus for his craft.

65. **(C)** Lake Lucerne is in Switzerland—Lake Michigan is in the United States; Lake Geneva is in Switzerland—Lake Okeechobee is in the United States.

66. **(C)** A musician in a concert knows what to play by referring to the score; an actor in a play knows what to act out by referring to the script.

67. **(D)** We associate smoke with a herring, a ham, a cigarette, a volcano.

68. **(C)** DDT is lethal to an insect; a knight is lethal to a dragon.

69. **(B)** Just as plywood is a variation of wood by man's intervention, so the nectarine is a variation of the peach.

70. **(D)** Partridges congregate in a covey—wasps in a nest.

71. **(A)** A lapidary may work with a ruby; a sculptor may work with alabaster.

72. **(B)** We speak of the warp and the woof—also rank and file.

73. **(B)** Although the four choices rhyme with *smile,* only *style* has a rhyming vowel not consistent with the others (whose rhyming vowel is *i*); the rhyming vowels of *schemes* and *dreams* differ.

74. **(A)** Forsook and drank are past tense forms; frozen and swum are participial forms.

75. **(B)** A sandal is a lighter version of footwear than a boot is; a hatchet is a smaller version of a sharp-edged instrument than an ax is.

76. **(B)** A centaur is half horse, half man; a satyr is half goat, half man.

77. **(D)** A cell is part of a battery; a shaft is part of a feather.

78. **(B)** *Gnat* is spelled correctly—*spagetti* is spelled incorrectly; *accommodation* is spelled correctly—*ecstacy* is spelled incorrectly.

79. **(B)** 30 days hath September, April, June, and November.

80. **(B)** Entry begins with an E—finest begins with the next letter in the alphabet (F); initiative begins with an I—jewelry begins with the next letter in the alphabet (J).

81. **(D)** *Frugal* and *prodigal* are antonyms—so are *disinterested* and *partial*. Note: the word prodigal does not, of itself, mean *wandering* even though we speak of the "prodigal son."

82. **(B)** Eiffel and Pisa are both towers; a schooner and a rowboat are both surface water vehicles.

83. **(D)** We speak of the weeping (mournful) willow and the mighty (sturdy) oak.

84. **(B)** Exhort means to urge on—a stronger version of advise; entice is a stronger version of tempt.

85. **(B)** When you weld steel, you consolidate pieces of it; when you purse your lips, you put them close together.

86. **(A)** Testimony is a statement about someone else—a confession is a statement about oneself; a biography is a writing about someone else—an autobiography about oneself.

87. **(B)** Mohammedanism was founded by an actual person (Mohammed) whom the belief was named after; the same situation applies to Buddhism, Zoroastrianism, and Confucianism.

88. **(B)** Both a lamb and a deer are timid; both a peacock and a lion are proud.

89. **(C)** A building, in part, consists of a foundation; a cat, in part, consists of fur.

90. **(A)** *Tele* is a Greek root meaning distance; *arch* is a Greek root meaning leader.

91. **(D)** A tattoo is an evening military signal—vespers are evening prayers; reveille is a morning military signal—matins are morning prayers.

92. **(C)** A person who is prostrate is in a position for yielding; a person who is supine is in a position for sleeping.

93. **(A)** A harpoon is used to catch a whale; a fly is a hook used to catch a trout.

94. **(D)** Skiing is a sport engaged in on snow—hockey on ice.

95. **(A)** The material of which a skeleton consists is bone; the material of which a tree consists is wood.

96. **(C)** A tine is part of a fork; a flange is part of a wheel.

97. **(D)** One's attire is brightened with some decoration; one's communication is brightened with wit.

98. **(A)** A spare, in bowling, is the knocking down of all pins with the two bowls—a strike is the knocking down of all pins with a single bowl; in baseball, a run is scored, more often, by two or more hits—a homerun is scored by a single hit.

99. **(B)** When wheat is threshed, the grain is separated from the useless husks; when water is distilled, the refined water is left after the useless substances have been removed.

100. **(B)** A sybarite is fun-loving (opposite of abstemious); a Spartan is laconic (opposite of garrulous).

ANSWER SHEET FOR SAMPLE MAT

	A	B	C	D		A	B	C	D		A	B	C	D		A	B	C	D
1					26					51					76				
2					27					52					77				
3					28					53					78				
4					29					54					79				
5					30					55					80				
6					31					56					81				
7					32					57					82				
8					33					58					83				
9					34					59					84				
10					35					60					85				

Make only ONE mark for each answer.   Additional and stray marks may be counted as mistakes.   In making corrections, erase errors COMPLETELY.

	A	B	C	D		A	B	C	D		A	B	C	D		A	B	C	D
11					36					61					86				
12					37					62					87				
13					38					63					88				
14					39					64					89				
15					40					65					90				
16					41					66					91				
17					42					67					92				
18					43					68					93				
19					44					69					94				
20					45					70					95				
21					46					71					96				
22					47					72					97				
23					48					73					98				
24					49					74					99				
25					50					75					100				

Miller Analogies Test

(Sample 3)

Time: 50 minutes

> *Directions:* From the four lettered words in parentheses, select that word which best completes the analogy which exists among the three capitalized words.

1. CHURCH : KIRK :: ENGLAND :
   (A. Scotland B. cathedral C. cork
   D. bishop)

2. SHAVE : (A. lather B. blade C. razor
   D. mirror) :: KNIFE : CUT

3. OXEN : STRENGTH :: (A. furnace
   B. animal C. assembly D. ant) :
   INDUSTRY

4. (A. rectify B. make C. find D. realize) :
   MISTAKE :: REGAIN : LOSS

5. SHIP : (A. crow's nest B. deck C. prow
   D. captain) :: COLUMN : CAPITAL

6.

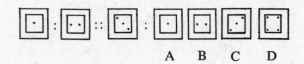

   A   B   C   D

7. CLEOPATRA : (A. Caesar B. poison
   C. Anthony D. beauty) :: GOLIATH :
   STONE

8. (A. circle B. heart C. dissemination
   D. artery) : CIRCULATE :: DITCH :
   IRRIGATE

9. BRIGHT : GAUDY :: (A. urged
   B. driven C. prevented D. acquiesced) :
   OBLIGED

10. STREAM : (A. grouch B. moor C. river
    D. strand) :: SALMON : GROUSE

11. EGO : ID :: SELF : (A. desire
    B. Rorschach C. conscience D. morality)

12. HIGH GEAR : (A. automobile B. driver
    C. speed D. brake) :: PROGRESS :
    RECESSION

13. (A. gem B. spore C. illegitimacy
    D. superficiality) : SPURIOUS :: MONEY
    : COUNTERFEIT

14. LANE : PLANETARIUM :: (A. way
    B. spirit C. élan D. cluster) :
    MELANCHOLY

15. 135 : 36 :: 253 : (A. 55 B. 54 C. 53
    D. 52)

16. QUEUE : (A. mop B. tail C. line
    D. broom) :: CUE : BROUGHAM

17. COLONEL : REGIMENT :: (A. major
    B. captain C. private D. general) :
    BATTALION

18. COMPOSITION : OUTLINE :: HOUSE :
    (A. silhouette B. builder C. roof
    D. blueprint)

19. (A. refreshing B. white C. icy D. flaky)
    : SNOW :: TALL : GIRAFFE

20. CASTE : CLASS :: APPOINTED :
    (A. status B. achieved C. between
    D. upper-middle)

21. INDEX : CONTENTS :: MATURITY :
    (A. adolescence B. infancy C. puberty
    D. adulthood)

22. OBSEQUIOUS : POLITE :: (A. direct
B. cruel   C. objective   D. candid) :
HARSH

23. SQUARE : (A. parallelogram   B. Trafalgar
C. poem   D. waltz) :: QUADRUPLET :
COUPLET

24. ROBE : (A. priest   B. state   C. hangman
D. court) :: SHIELD : COMMUNITY

25. (A. m   B. p   C. t   D. l) : H :: W : S

26. CHOLERIC : PHLEGMATIC ::
(A. timid   B. blind   C. mute
D. temerarious) : CIRCUMSPECT

27. IRON : (A. hard   B. strong   C. steel
D. pig) :: OIL : CRUDE

28. (A. astronomy   B. play   C. symphony
D. heavens) : STAR :: CONCERTO :
SOLOIST

29. DOOR : (A. key   B. knock   C. jamb
D. room) :: TELEPHONE : RING

30. NOISE : JACKHAMMER :: (A. cup
B. knife   C. saddle   D. manuscript) :
SRIVENER

31. FAULTY : USELESS :: SLOW :
(A. moronic   B. intelligent   C. wary
D. fresh)

32. HEDGER : SHRUBBERY :: (A. snuffer
B. cougher   C. whittler   D. stickler) :
STICK

33. (A. slot   B. note   C. band   D. harmony) :
VALVE :: HARMONICA : TRUMPET

34. FLAUNT : (A. destructively   B. stupidly
C. willingly   D. boastfully) :: BETRAY :
DECEPTIVELY

35. HOUYHNHNM : YAHOO :: REASON :
(A. learning   B. intelligence   C. ignorance
D. genius)

36. DEFIED : ASTRIDE :: EARTH :
(A. geography   B. zoölogy   C. birth
D. life)

37. ISTANBUL : CONSTANTINOPLE ::
(A. Stalingrad   B. Leningrad   C. Moscow
D. Odessa) : ST. PETERSBURG

38. (A. 1899   B. 1900   C. 1901   D. 1902) :
1910 :: 1950 : 1959

39. DUNGEON : (A. torture   B. prison
C. castle   D. guard) :: CELLAR : HOME

40. ABRASIVE : SANDPAPER :: (A. costly
B. beautiful   C. smooth   D. Oriental) :
SILK

41. AUTOMOBILE : COUPE :: BOAT :
(A. trawler   B. freighter   C. yacht   D. tug)

42. SHEEP : COUNT :: (A. wager
B. account   C. choice   D. bet) : PLACE

43. MAN : (A. bird   B. centipede   C. elephant
D. Adam) :: WHEELBARROW :
BICYCLE

44. (A. scoff   B. insult   C. ridicule   D. attack)
: DERISION :: FLEE : TERROR

45. CANTON : COUNTY :: (A. Ohio
B. Japan   C. Switzerland   D. Russia) :
IRELAND

46. (A. kilogram   B. chain   C. peck
D. transit) : SURVEYOR :: CARAT :
JEWELER

47. BORROWER : BEGGAR :: (A. lender
B. security   C. loan   D. repayment) :
GIFT

48. PEN : (A. cover   B. point   C. pencil
D. ink) ::   BIT   : BRACE

49. SHERRY : BEER :: PORT :
(A. champagne   B. sauterne   C. claret
D. muscatel)

50. HONOR : GOVERNOR :: (A. Excellency
B. Majesty   C. Highness   D. Grace) :
DUKE

51. ANDIRON : PEDESTAL :: (A. log
B. bucket   C. anvil   D. skillet) :
STATUE

52. GENERAL : STARS :: COLONEL :
(A. oak   B. silver   C. gold   D. eagle)

53. (A. insist   B. reply   C. demur   D. demand)
: REFUSE :: LAZY : INERT

54. COD : SEINE :: MAY : (A. Suez
B. Hatteras   C. Atlantic   D. Missouri)

55. INCOGNITO : (A. detail   B. combatant
C. caricature   D. conjugal) ::
DISCHARGE : ADULT

56. POOL : SHOOT :: (A. Cain   B. Eve
C. Joshua   D. Hannah) : PRAISE

57. FELONY : MISDEMEANOR :: SIN :
(A. piccalilli   B. picayune   C. peccadillo
D. picador)

58. NOSE : (A. calf   B. chest   C. thigh
D. knuckle) :: CHIN : ELBOW

59. (A. boloney   B. tomato juice   C. roast
chicken   D. shrimp salad) : APPLE
PIE :: ANTLERS : HOOVES

60. IBLE : ABLE :: TON : (A. acy   B. cry
C. wich   D. itis)

61. MAST : SLOOP :: (A. filament
B. socket   C. light   D. lamp) : BULB

62. SERIOUS : (A. laconic   B. garrulous
C. deaf   D. puzzled) :: HUNGRY :
IMPECUNIOUS

63. (A. lighthouse   B. cumbersome
C. plumbing   D. spine) : DENMARK ::
VICTORY : WARDEN

64. SYRACUSE : (A. Rochester   B. Geneva
C. Binghamton   D. Goshen) ::
CARTHAGE : ROME

65. PALL : CLOY :: (A. obbligato
B. innuendo   C. declaration   D. crescendo)
: INSINUATION

66. ORGANISM : (A. plant   B. animal
C. bacteria   D. cell) :: LIGHT : WAVE

67. KOLN : WEIN :: COLOGNE :
(A. Vienna   B. Prague   C. Warsaw
D. Hamburg)

68. SEDIMENT : DIME :: (A. discussion
B. debate   C. argument   D. rally) : GUM

69. SAXOPHONE : (A. harp   B. sandwich
C. distance   D. bag) :: HANSOM :
MACADAM

70. BUTTERFLY : (A. insect   B. silkworm
C. wings   D. summer) :: CHRYSALIS
: COCOON

71. ICELAND : NORWAY :: (A. winter
B. thorns   C. president   D. sovereign) :
CROWN

72. (A. discourse   B. plot   C. Olympics
D. Greek) : PLATO :: TEAM :
MANET

73. CYLINDER :   MOTOR   ::
FOUNDATION : (A. plan   B. house
C. brick   D. basis)

74. BANANA : (A. sapphire   B. saltceller
C. stone   D. tree) :: BUTTER : SKY

75. GNASH : TEETH :: (A. fold   B. clasp
C. gnarl   D. wring) : HANDS

76. (A. opossum   B. fox   C. beaver   D. lady)
: KANGAROO :: CHICKEN :
COCKROACH

77. QUESTION MARK : COLON ::
SEMICOLON : (A. dash   B. parentheses
C. hyphen   D. comma)

78. (A. roast   B. grill   C. bake   D. boil) :
CLAM :: FRY : FISH

79. CLARINET : PIANO :: WIND :
(A. string   B. wood   C. percussion
D. pianist)

80. ELEVATOR : SKYSCRAPER ::
(A. escalator   B. companionway
C. bulkhead   D. bridge) : SHIP

81. PROPENSITY : (A. riches   B. weight
C. bias   D. thought) :: BAT : CLUB

82. SALZBURG : STRATFORD ::
(A. Connecticut   B. Avon   C. Mozart
D. Germany) : SHAKESPEARE

83. FLAMMABLE : INFLAMMABLE ::
PERTINENT : (A. impertinent
B. inopportune   C. incoherent   D. relative)

84. (A. revolution   B. dance   C. torque
D. axis) : ROTATE :: FRICTION :
RESIST

85. PRISM : (A. spectrum   B. reflection
C. light   D. binoculars) :: FAMINE :
WANT

86. LOOP : HUB :: BEEF : (A. corn
B. beans   C. tobacco   D. cotton)

87. JANUARY : (A. Cleveland   B. Cincinnati
C. Washington   D. Seattle) :: SUNDAY :
JUPITER

88. LIFT : ELEVATOR :: (A. oil   B. grease
C. gas   D. petrol) : GASOLINE

89. (A. wall   B. posse   C. antic   D. hose) :
BLAST :: NOTARY : OPTIMISM

90. TORT : LITIGATION :: CONTRACT :
(A. signature   B. obligation   C. clause
D. equity)

91. BULL : (A. wolf   B. turtle   C. fish
D. snail) :: CRAB : LION

92. EVIL : LIVE :: WOLF : (A. sheep
B. good   C. flow   D. worry)

93. FILIGREE : METAL :: (A. lace
B. linen   C. cotton   D. silk) : THREAD

94. GARROTING : DEATH :: FRICTION :
(A. rubbing   B. lubricant   C. heat
D. slaughter)

95. (A. philosophy   B. territory   C. mountain
D. restaurant) : INSINCERITY ::
SLAVERY : LOVE

96. SICKLE : RUSSIA :: (A. scythe
B. crescent   C. Caspian   D. Dardanelles) :
TURKEY

97. CICERO : DEMOSTHENES ::
ROOSEVELT : (A. MacArthur
B. Hemingway   C. Shaw   D. Churchill)

98. MINUTE : (A. steak   B. hour
C. second   D. immensity) :: PAGE :
BOOK

99. COKE : COAL :: (A. firewood
B. planks   C. saw   D. lumberjack) :
TIMBER

100. SHOE   (A. fly   B. cobbler   C. pair
D. bell) : SAW :: GEAR

END OF MILLER ANALOGIES TEST (SAMPLE 3)

Answer Sheet

(Answer grid — questions 1–100, each with bubbles labeled a, b, c, d, e; all blank)

Correct Answers For The Foregoing Questions

(Please make every effort to answer the questions on your own before looking at these answers. You'll make faster progress by following this rule.)

1. A	15. A	27. D	39. C	51. A	63. B	75. D	87. C
2. B	16. D	28. B	40. C	52. D	64. D	76. A	88. D
3. D	17. A	29. B	41. C	53. C	65. B	77. B	89. C
4. A	18. D	30. D	42. D	54. D	66. D	78. C	90. B
5. A	19. B	31. A	43. C	55. A	67. A	79. C	91. C
6. D	20. B	32. C	44. A	56. A	68. C	80. B	92. C
7. B	21. B	33. A	45. C	57. C	69. B	81. D	93. A
8. D	22. B	34. D	46. B	58. D	70. B	82. C	94. C
9. A	23. D	35. C	47. C	59. B	71. C	83. D	95. A
10. B	24. D	36. C	48. A	60. C	72. B	84. C	96. B
11. A	25. D	37. B	49. A	61. A	73. B	85. A	97. D
12. D	26. D	38. C	50. D	62. A	74. A	86. B	98. B
13. A							99. B
14. C							100. D

EXPLANATION OF ANSWERS FOR MAT SAMPLE TEST 3

1. **(A)** The English say church; the Scotch say kirk.

2. **(B)** One shaves with a blade (which is sharp); one cuts with a knife (which is sharp).

3. **(D)** We associate ants with industry; we associate oxen with strength.

4. **(A)** In both cases, you improve a poor or unfortunate condition: you rectify a mistake and you regain a loss.

5. **(A)** The crow's nest is the small observation platform near the top of a ship's mast; the capital is the upper part of a column.

6. **(D)** The second square has one more dot than the first square. Therefore, the correct answer is alternative D which has one more dot than the third square.

7. **(B)** Cleopatra died from the poison bite of an asp; Goliath was slain by a stone hurled from a sling.

8. **(D)** Blood is circulated by means of an artery; water is supplied (irrigated) by means of a ditch.

9. **(A)** When something is gaudy, it is objectionably bright; when you are obliged, you are not only urged—you are compelled. We are dealing with a question of degree here.

10. **(B)** The natural habitat of salmon is a stream —of grouse is a moor.

11. **(A)** Ego is a psychological term for self; id is a psychological term for desire.

12. **(D)** For greater speed, you use high gear— to arrest speed, you use a brake; progress and recession are, likewise, opposite in meaning.

13. **(A)** A gem is worthless when it is spurious; money is worthless when it is counterfeit.

14. **(C)** The letters of *lane* are the second, third, fourth, and fifth letters of *planetarium;* the letters of *elan* are the second, third, fourth, and fifth letters of *melancholy.*

15. **(A)** Consider 135: the hundreds number (1) and the unit number (5) add up to 6 . . . 6 is the unit number of 36; Consider 253: the hundreds number (2) and the unit number (3) add up to 5 . . . 5 is the unit number of 55.

16. **(D)** Queue and cue are pronounced the same—so are broom and brougham.

17. **(A)** A colonel leads a regiment; a major leads a battalion.

18. **(D)** You follow the outline to write a composition; you follow the blueprint to construct a house.

19. **(B)** White is more closely associated with snow than the other choices are; tall is associated with giraffe.

20. **(B)** Caste and class are the same parts of speech (nouns) and both begin with the same letter (*c*); appointed and achieved are the same parts of speech (verbs) and both begin with the same letter (*a*).

21. **(B)** The index comes at the end of a book —the table of contents at the beginning; maturity comes in the latter part of life—infancy at the beginning.

22. **(B)** A person who is overpolite is likely to be obsequious; a person who is overharsh is likely to be cruel.

23. **(D)** A square has four sides—a waltz is danced by a pair; a quadruplet is a combination of four things—a couplet consists of two successive rhyming lines of verse.

24. **(D)** A robe is worn by a judge in court as a sign of authority; a shield is worn by a policeman in his community as a sign of authority.

25. **(D)** In the alphabet, *l* is the fourth letter after *h*; *w* is the fourth letter after *s*.

26. **(D)** Choleric and phlegmatic are opposites; so are temerarious and circumspect.

27. **(D)** Oil in its rough state is called crude oil; iron in its rough state is called pig iron.

28. **(B)** The star takes the leading role in a play just as the soloist takes the leading role in a concert.

29. **(B)** You proceed to open the door when you hear a knock; you proceed to answer the telephone when you hear a ring.

30. **(D)** A jackhammer is a rock-drilling machine that makes considerable noise; a scrivener is a copyist—therefore, one who makes a manuscript.

31. **(A)** If something is quite faulty, it is useless; if a person is extremely slow, he is probably moronic.

32. **(C)** A hedger trims shrubbery; a whittler slices off the outside of a stick.

33. **(A)** Blowing into the slots produces the harmonica pitch; pressing the valves produces the trumpet pitch.

34. **(D)** When one flaunts, he conducts himself in a boastful manner; when one betrays, he conducts himself in a deceptive manner.

35. **(C)** In "Gulliver's Travels" by Jonathan Swift, the Houyhnhnms symbolized intelligence—the Yahoos, stupidity; reason and ignorance are opposites.

36. **(C)** Defied rhymes with astride; earth rhymes with birth.

37. **(B)** Istanbul was formerly called Constantinople; Leningrad was formerly called St. Petersburg.

38. **(C)** The differences between 1901 and 1910 is nine years; between 1950 and 1959, nine years.

39. **(C)** A dungeon is the underground portion of a castle; a cellar is the underground portion of a home.

40. **(C)** Sandpaper is abrasive; silk is smooth.

41. **(C)** A coupe is a car that is usually used for personal use; a yacht is a boat used for private pleasure.

42. **(D)** You count sheep and you place a bet.

43. **(C)** A man has two legs—an elephant has twice as many; a wheelbarrow has one wheel —a bicycle has twice as many.

44. **(A)** One who scoffs shows derision; one who flees shows terror.

45. **(C)** Switzerland is divided into cantons; Ireland is divided into counties.

46. **(B)** A chain is a measuring instrument used in surveying; a caret is a unit of weight used by a jeweler.

47. **(C)** You give a loan to a borrower—a gift to a beggar.

48. **(A)** A pen fits into its cover; a bit fits into a brace.

49. **(A)** Sherry has no carbonation—beer has carbonation; port has no carbonation—champagne has carbonation.

50. **(D)** It's His Honor, the Governor and His Grace, the Duke.

51. **(A)** An andiron is used to hold logs; a pedestal (as a base) holds a statue.

52. **(D)** Stars on the uniform shoulder signify the status of a general; an eagle in the same place indicates colonel status.

53. **(C)** Refusing is an extreme form of demurring; being inert is an extreme form of laziness.

54. **(D)** Cape Cod—Seine River—Cape May—Missouri River.

55. **(A)** The preferred pronunciation stress of these four words—incognito, detail, discharge, adult—is on the second syllable, although other pronunciations of these words are permissible.

56. **(A)** Pool and shoot have the same vowel sound; so do Cain and praise.

57. **(C)** A misdemeanor is an offense which is less serious than a felony; a peccadillo is a trifling sin.

58. **(D)** The nose, knuckle, chin, and elbow all protrude.

59. **(B)** Tomato juice is commonly drunk to start a meal—apple pie is often eaten to end a meal (as a dessert); the antlers of a deer constitute the highest part of the animal—the hooves, the lowest part.

60. **(C)** *ible* and *able* are suffixes meaning able; *ton* and *wich* are suffixes referring to towns.

61. **(A)** A mast is part of a sloop; a filament is part of a bulb.

62. **(A)** A person who is laconic is likely to be serious; a person who is impecunious is likely to be hungry.

63. **(B)** Cumbersome, Denmark, victory, and warden each contain the letter "*r*."

64. **(D)** All of the cities listed are in New York State. However, only Syracuse, Goshen, Carthage, and Rome are named after cities of ancient vintage.

65. **(B)** Pall and cloy are synonyms; innuendo and insinuation are also synonyms.

66. **(D)** An organism is made up of cells; light consists physically of waves.

67. **(A)** The German name for Cologne is Koln —for Vienna, Wien.

68. **(C)** Dime is part of the word sediment; gum is part of the word argument.

69. **(B)** A saxophone and a sandwich were named after inventors—so were a hansom (cab) and a macadam (road).

70. **(B)** An early stage in the development of the butterfly is the chrysalis; an early stage in the development of the silkworm is the cocoon.

71. **(C)** Iceland, as a republic, is headed by a president; Norway, as a monarchy, is ruled by a king (crown).

72. **(B)** The word Plato is made up of the four letters of *plot* (plus one more letter); Manet is made up of the four letters of *team* (plus one more letter).

73. **(B)** A cylinder is part of a motor; a foundation is part of a house.

74. **(A)** A yellow (butter) banana—a blue (sapphire) sky.

75. **(D)** In anger or dismay, you may gnash your teeth or wring your hands.

76. **(A)** The opossum and the kangaroo are marsupial; the chicken and the cockroach are oviparous.

77. **(B)** Each of the following punctuation marks consists of two discrete markings: question mark, colon, semicolon, parentheses.

78. **(C)** Types of picnics are the clambake and the fishfry.

79. **(C)** A clarinet is a wind instrument—a piano is a percussion instrument.

80. **(B)** An elevator is used to go to the top of a skyscraper; a companionway is used to get to the deck of a ship.

81. **(C)** A propensity is a leaning in a certain direction—a bias is a strong leaning; a bat is not as ominous as a club. We have here a question of degree.

82. **(C)** Salzburg was the birthplace of Mozart; Stratford was the birthplace of Shakespeare.

83. **(D)** Flammable and inflammable are synonyms; so are pertinent and relative.

84. **(C)** A torque causes rotation; friction causes resistance.

85. **(A)** A spectrum is created by a prism; want is created by a famine.

86. **(B)** The Loop and the Hub are nicknames for Chicago and Boston respectively; Chicago is known for its beef—Boston for its beans.

87. **(C)** We have a number of "firsts" here: January—first month; Washington—first president; Sunday—first day of the week; Jupiter —first planet in size.

88. **(D)** The English say lift for elevator and petrol for gasoline.

89. **(C)** Antic contains the letter *t*; so do blast, notary, and optimism.

90. **(B)** A tort is a wrong that entails litigation; a contract entails obligation.

91. **(C)** The bull (taurus), fish (pisces), crab (cancer), and lion (leo) are signs of the zodiac.

92. **(C)** *Live* is *evil* spelled backwards; *flow* is *wolf* spelled backwards.

93. **(A)** Filigree is delicate ornamental openwork made of metal; lace is delicate openwork fabric made from thread.

94. **(C)** Garroting commonly causes death; friction commonly causes heat.

95. **(A)** Philosophy and insincerity are both abstract nouns; so are slavery and love.

96. **(B)** The sickle (and hammer) is a symbol of Russian power; the crescent is a symbol of Turkish power.

97. **(D)** Cicero and Demosthenes were orators; Roosevelt and Churchill were statesmen.

98. **(B)** A minute is a unit of an hour; a page is a unit of a book.

99. **(B)** Coke is obtained by heating coal—there is some waste; planks are formed by cutting timber—there is some waste.

100. **(D)** A shoe and a bell have a tongue; a saw and a gear have teeth.

PART FOUR

Nonverbal Analogy Tests
Reasoning Ability Practice

Final Advice

4

Practice Using Answer Sheets

Alter numbers to match the practice and drill questions in each part of the book.
Make only ONE mark for each answer. Additional and stray marks may be counted as mistakes.
In making corrections, erase errors COMPLETELY. Make glossy black marks.

FOUR NONVERBAL ANALOGY TESTS

FIGURE ANALOGIES TEST ONE

DIRECTIONS: In this type of test, each problem consists of two groups of figures labeled 1 and 2. These two groups are followed by five answer figures, lettered A, B, C, D, and E. For each problem you must decide what characteristic each of the figures in Group 1 has that none of the figures in Group 2 has. Then select the lettered answer figure that has this characteristic.

S1207

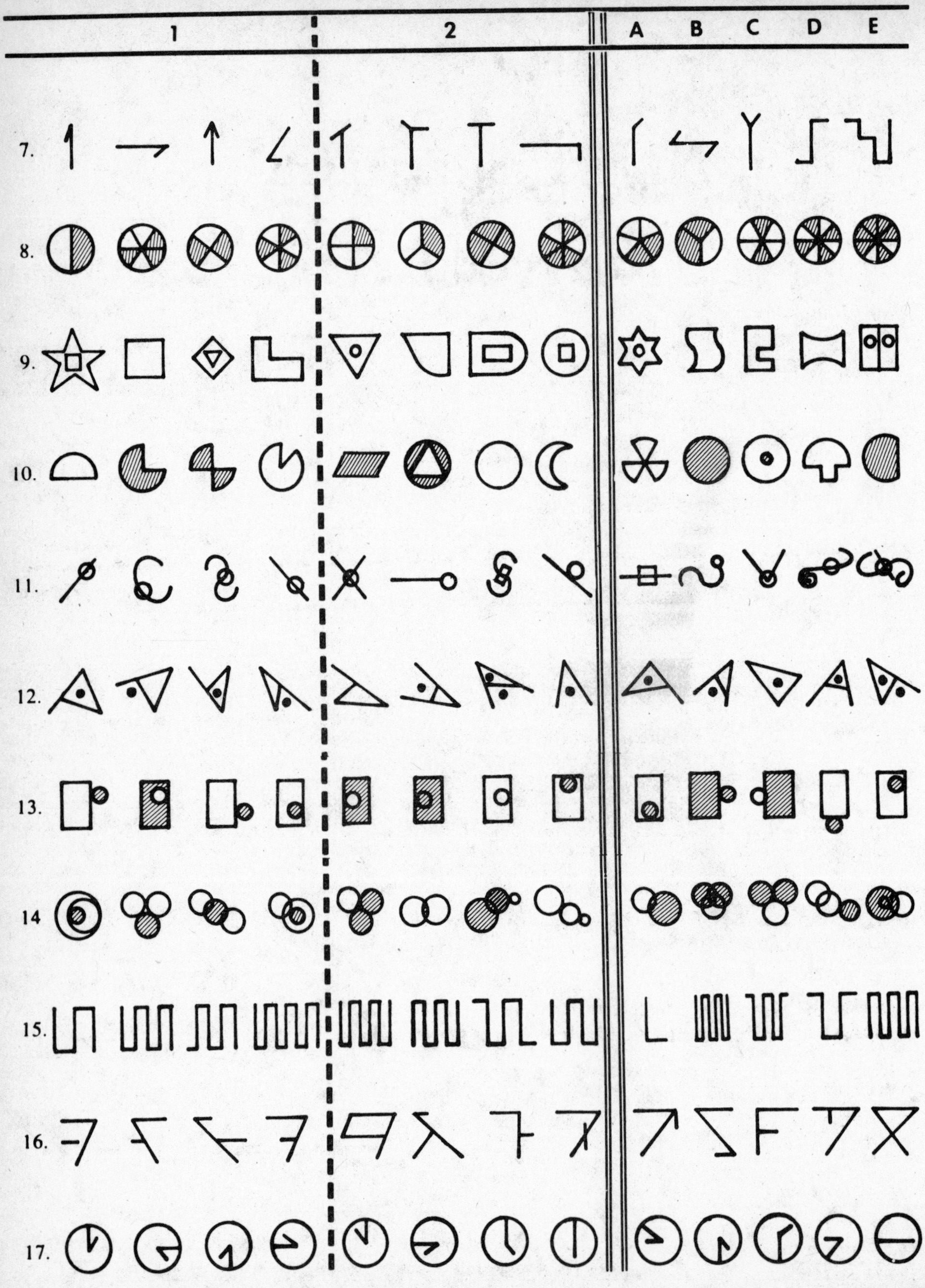
1
2
A B C D E
7.
8.
9.
10.
11.
12.
13.
14
15.
16.
17.

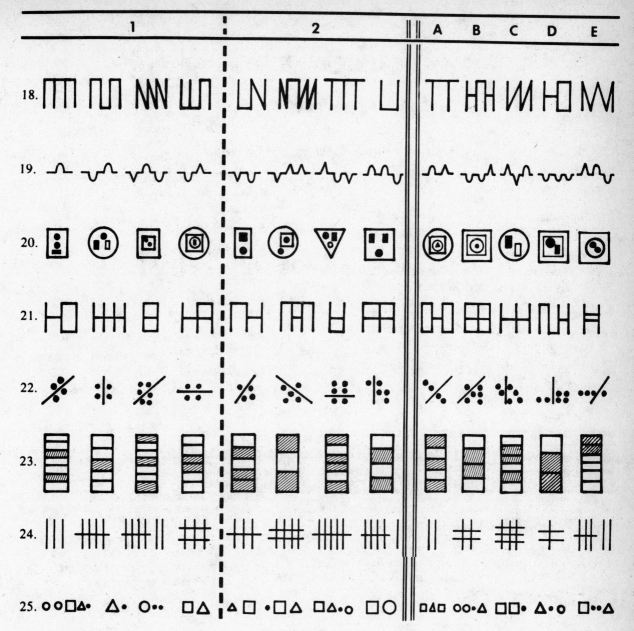

END OF SECTION

If you finish before the allotted time is up, check your work on this section only. When time is up, proceed directly to the next section and do not return to this section.

EXPLANATORY ANSWERS

TEST ONE

Every figure in Group I, but no figure in Group II...

1. (B)...has a point on top.
2. (C)...contains a forward "S" (which may be on its side, but not a mirror image).
3. (A)...has a dot above.
4. (C)...consists of a single white figure in the center of a shaded figure.
5. (E)...includes one vertical line.
6. (D)...is a *single* figure (of any color or shape) on a white background.
7. (B)...includes no right or obtuse angles (only acute angles).
8. (D)...is divided equally between white and black area.
9. (C)...includes only straight lines.
10. (A)...is a circle with "pie-shaped" sector(s) removed.
11. (D)...is a circle with a line or curve running completely through it.
12. (A)...is a triangle with one side extended, and one dot anywhere.
13. (E)...is a rectangle with a different-colored circle attached to its rightmost side.

14. (D)...consists of two white circles and one shaded circle.
15. (E)...ends on a down stroke: ⌐ (at the rightmost end).
16. (B)...consists of two horizontal lines and one diagonal line.
17. (D)...has an acute angle going *clockwise* from the long "hand" to the short one.
18. (B)...includes four (and only four) vertical lines.
19. (C)...has no two adjacent protrusions on the same side of the line.
20. (B)...consists of two circles and two rectangles (only).
21. (D)...has three horizontal lengths (between verticals).
22. (A)...has the same number of dots on each side of the line.
23. (E)...has more white boxes than shaded ones.
24. (D)...has an odd number of lines.
25. (C)...has the parts arranged so that all circles come to the left of everything else, all squares come to the left of triangles and dots, and all triangles precede dots.

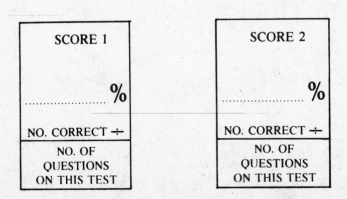

SCORE 1	SCORE 2
.... %	.... %
NO. CORRECT ÷	NO. CORRECT ÷
NO. OF QUESTIONS ON THIS TEST	NO. OF QUESTIONS ON THIS TEST

FIGURE ANALOGIES TEST TWO

20 minutes

DIRECTIONS: Each of these problems consists of two groups of figures, labeled 1 and 2. These are followed by five lettered answer figures. For each problem you are to decide what characteristic each of the figures in group 1 has that none of the figures in group 2 has. Then select the lettered answer figure that has this characteristic.

	1	2	A B C D E

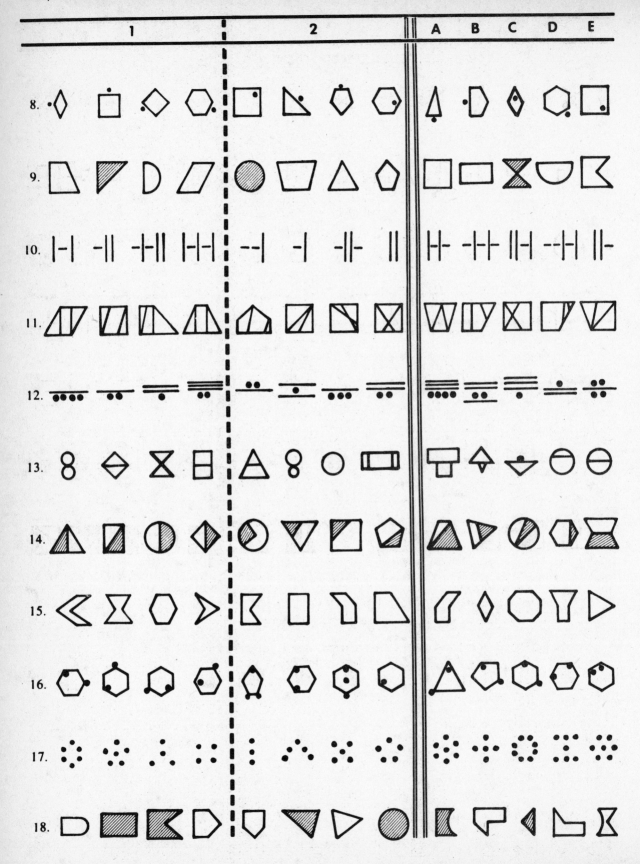

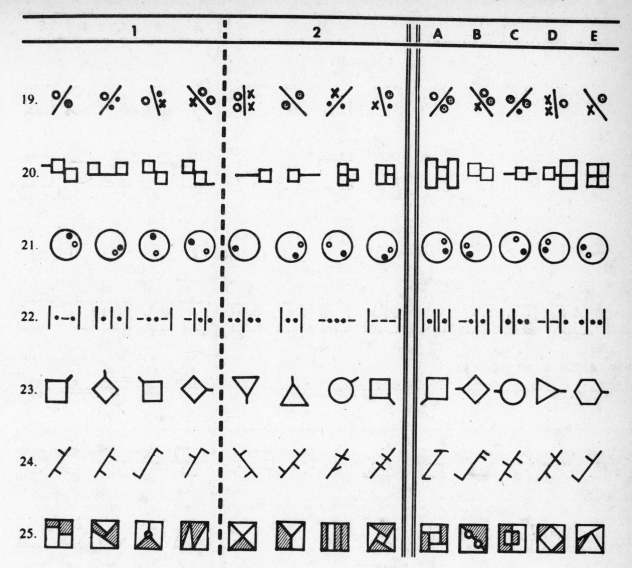

END OF SECTION

If you finish before the allotted time is up, check your work on
this section only. When time is up, proceed directly to the next
section and do not return to this section.

EXPLANATORY ANSWERS

TEST TWO

Every figure in Group I, but no figure in Group II...

1. **(C)** consists of three lines and three dots.

2. **(D)** consists of a single undivided shaded region touching any number of white regions.

3. **(B)** is a circle with three radii, two solid and one dotted such that two angles are formed totaling 180°

4. **(B)** contains intersections in the middle of its leftmost and rightmost vertical lines.

5. **(D)** has three elements, the first and third being mirror images.

6. **(A)** has exactly one dot to the right of the line.

7. **(C)** has more white area than shaded area.

8. **(D)** has an even number of sides, with the dot outside the figure.

9. **(E)** is *a*symmetrical if a vertical line is drawn through the center.

10. **(E)** has one more vertical line than the number of horizontal lines.

11. **(D)** consists of one quadrilateral inscribed inside another quadrilateral.

12. **(A)** has an odd number of elements, with no dot above any line.

13. **(E)** consists of two congruent parts.

14. **(E)** has equal areas of white and shaded territory.

15. **(B)** has no vertical lines.

16. **(C)** is a hexagon with one dot inside and one dot outside.

17. **(C)** has an even number of dots.

18. **(A)** has ⌐ at its leftmost end.

19. **(E)** has two elements to the right of the line and one to the left of it (a dot in a circle together count as two elements).

20. **(B)** has two rectangles.

21. **(E)** has the black dot above the white dot.

22. **(B)** contains five parts, two of which are dots.

23. **(B)** is a quadrilateral with a line attached to it and extending horizontally, straight up, or diagonally up.

24. **(E)** is a line slanted like this ╱ , with two perpendicular lines attached to it.

25. **(C)** consists of two shaded regions and two white ones.

SCORE 1
.... %
NO. CORRECT
NO. OF QUESTIONS ON THIS TEST

SCORE 2
.... %
NO. CORRECT
NO. OF QUESTIONS ON THIS TEST

FIGURE ANALOGIES TEST THREE

20 Minutes

DIRECTIONS: Each of these problems consists of two groups of figures, labeled 1 and 2. These are followed by five lettered answer figures. For each problem you are to decide what characteristic each of the figures in group 1 has that none of the figures in group 2 has. Then select the lettered answer figure that has this characteristic.

S1207

	1	2	A B C D E

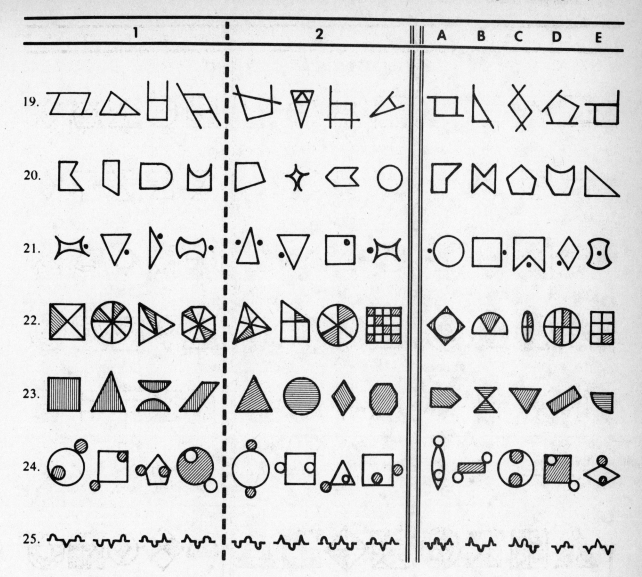

19.

20.

21.

22.

23.

24.

25.

END OF SECTION

If you finish before the allotted time is up, work on this part only.
When time is up, proceed directly to the next part and do not
return to this part.

EXPLANATORY ANSWERS

TEST THREE

Every figure in Group I, but no figure in Group II...

1. **(D)**...includes an upward angle made by a solid line and a dotted line.

2. **(A)**...has the dot on the right side when the V is rotated clockwise.

3. **(D)**...has three different figures, one inside the other without touching.

4. **(B)**...has four white regions, two shaded ones, two black ones.

5. **(C)**...has an equal number of white and/or black dots on either side of the line.

6. **(A)**...has three horizontal lines.

7. **(E)**...has two lines attached inside and one line outside.

8. **(E)**...has two two dots inside the figure.

9. **(B)**...has a dotted line crossing over a solid line.

10. **(B)**...includes at least one shaded triangle.

11. **(E)**...consists of a triangle, two circles, and a dot.

12. **(D)**...has four lines.

13. **(C)**...has an odd number of dots.

14. **(E)**...contains at least one empty white circle.

15. **(B)**...is a solid figure with one triangular piece cut off by a dotted line.

16. **(B)**...includes a semicircle (with its diameter) and a triangle.

17. **(C)**...has a figure, inside of which is one different type of figure (consider a dot a figure).

18. **(C)**...can be drawn with only four straight lines.

19. **(A)**...is a quadrilateral with only two opposite sides extended.

20. **(A)**...includes three sides of a rectangle.

21. **(B)**...has only one dot which is to the right of the main figure.

22. **(C)**...is one-quarter shaded in area.

23. **(D)**...has vertical shading.

24. **(D)**...has one circle inside, and one outside attached at opposite ends of the main figure; circles must be of a color different from the main figure.

25. **(C)**...has two curved humps and one pointed one.

SCORE 1	SCORE 2
..........................%	..........................%
NO. CORRECT	NO. CORRECT
NO. OF QUESTIONS ON THIS TEST	NO. OF QUESTIONS ON THIS TEST

FIGURE ANALOGIES TEST FOUR

20 Minutes

DIRECTIONS: Each of these problems consists of two groups of figures, labeled 1 and 2. These are followed by five lettered answer figures. For each problem you are to decide what characteristic each of the figures in group 1 has that none of the figures in group 2 has. Then select the lettered answer figure that has this characteristic.

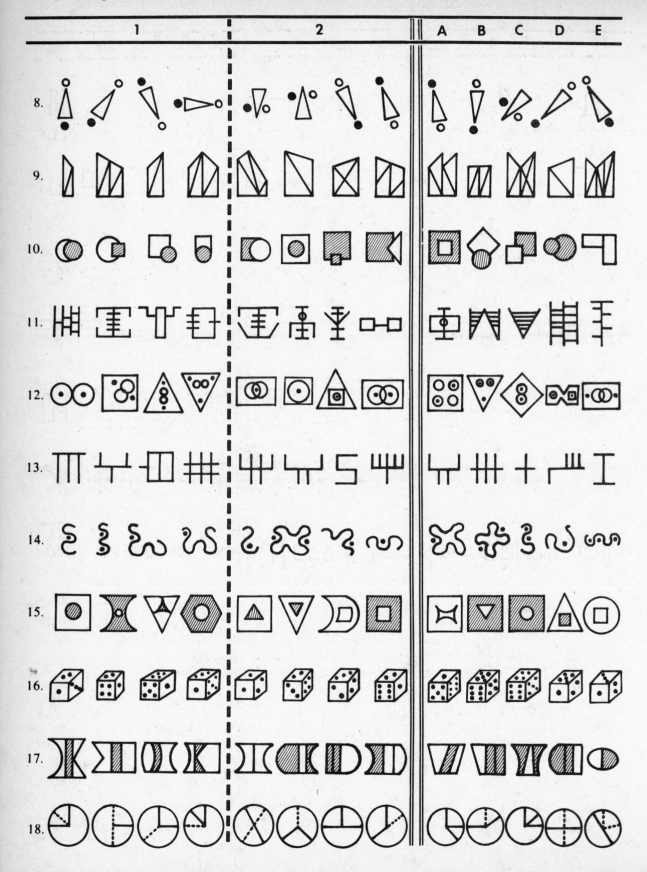

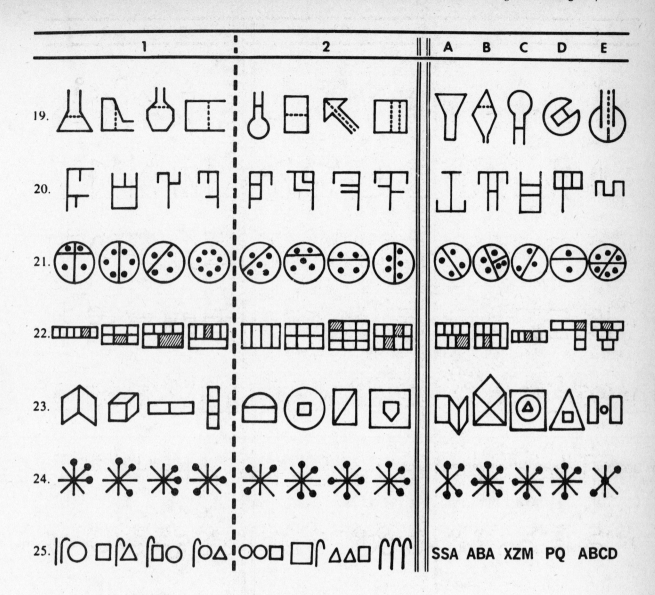

SSA   ABA   XZM   PQ   ABCD

END OF SECTION V

If you finish before the allotted time is up, work on this part only.
When time is up, proceed directly to the next part and do not
return to this part.

EXPLANATORY ANSWERS

TEST FOUR

Every figure in Group I, but no figure in Group II...

1. **(C)** ends at right with L .

2. **(E)** has four horizontal lines (between vertical lines) and four vertical lines.

3. **(A)** can be transformed to a rectangle by "cutting along the lines and rearranging the pieces."

4. **(E)** has an odd number (if we add the sum of the sides plus the dots).

5. **(D)** has twice as many dots to the right of the line as to the left (ignore circles).

6. **(E)** has a number of dots divisible by three.

7. **(B)** is composed of five lines.

8. **(E)** has its point toward a white circle and its base toward a black circle.

9. **(B)** has all internal diagonals slanted in this direction: / .

10. **(B)** consists of a shaded figure overlapping the side of a white figure.

11. **(E)** has six horizontal lines.

12. **(C)** includes two circles which intersect at no more than one point.

13. **(B)** has three vertical lines.

14. **(A)** has dots only to the left of the main figure.

15. **(C)** consists of a *curved* figure inside another figure of a different shape and color.

16. **(C)** is a possible view of a common die which looks like this unfolded:

17. **(A)** consists of two white regions surrounding a black one.

18. **(B)** consists of three radii in a circle, such that at least one radius is solid, and at least one dotted, and at least one pair of radii form a right angle.

19. **(B)** contains a region separated from the outside only by a dotted line.

20. **(A)** can be drawn with two horizontal lines and three vertical lines.

21. **(D)** has an odd number of dots in each region of the circle that is separated by lines, or in the whole circle itself if there are no lines.

22. **(E)** is divided into six regions, one of which is shaded.

23. **(A)** consists solely of parallelograms.

24. **(C)** has three dots, none on the same line.

25. **(C)** has a trio of different symbols.

PATTERN ANALYSIS AND COMPREHENSION

17 practice exercises. Important variations
on a significant test theme in spatial relations and
aptitude exams.

Visualizing Figures

IN questions like these, which are given on tests like yours, you are required to select one of the drawings of objects (A), (B), (C), or (D) below, that could be made from the flat piece drawn at the left, if this flat piece were folded on the dotted lines shown in the drawing.

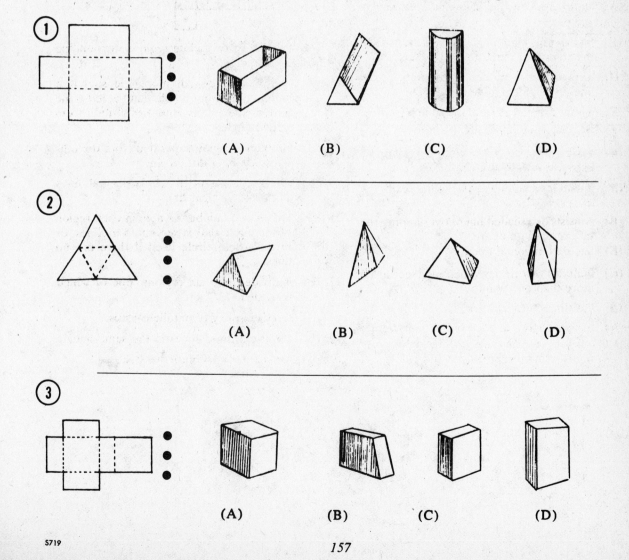

1

(A)   (B)   (C)   (D)

2

(A)   (B)   (C)   (D)

3

(A)   (B)   (C)   (D)

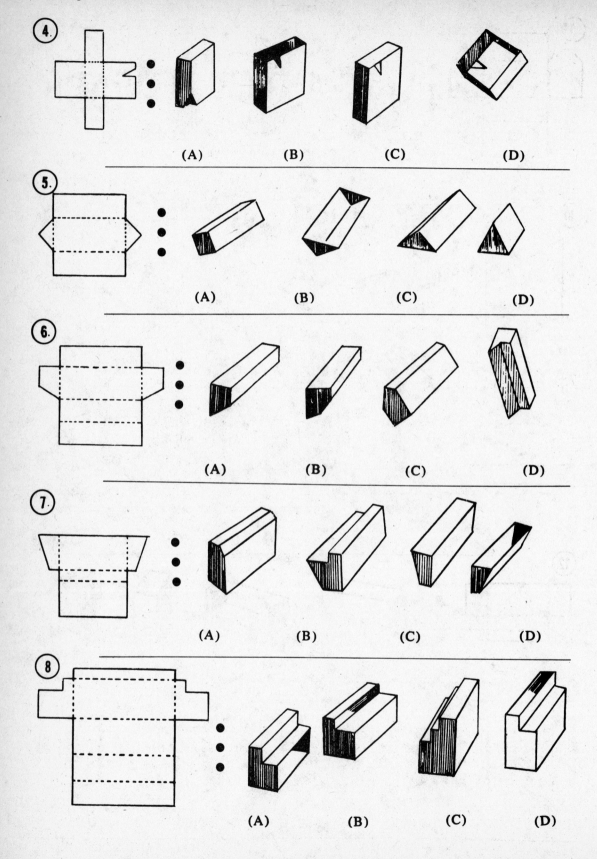

4.

(A)   (B)   (C)   (D)

5.

(A)   (B)   (C)   (D)

6.

(A)   (B)   (C)   (D)

7.

(A)   (B)   (C)   (D)

8.

(A)   (B)   (C)   (D)

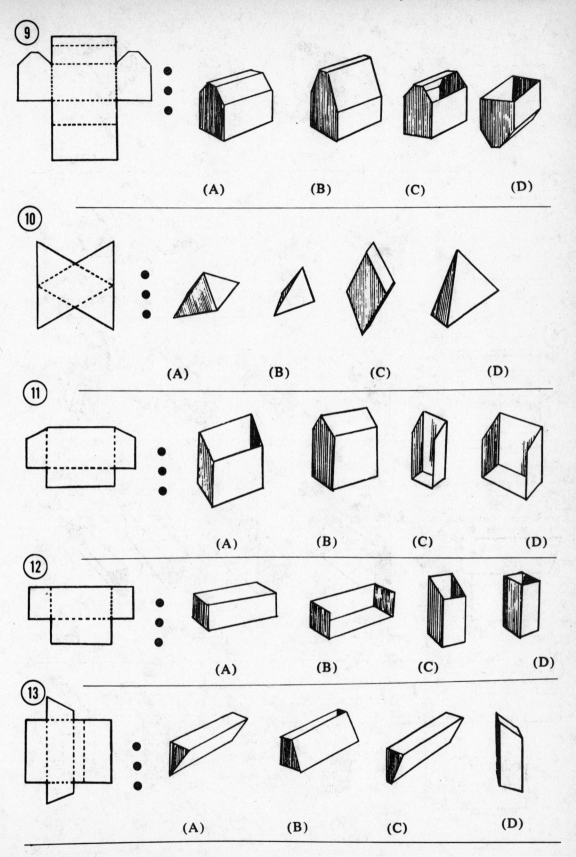

⑨

(A) (B) (C) (D)

⑩

(A) (B) (C) (D)

⑪

(A) (B) (C) (D)

⑫

(A) (B) (C) (D)

⑬

(A) (B) (C) (D)

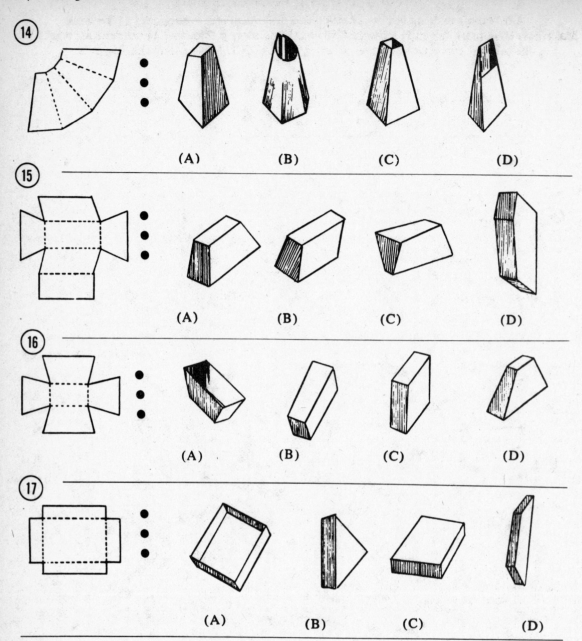

(14)

(A)   (B)   (C)   (D)

(15)

(A)   (B)   (C)   (D)

(16)

(A)   (B)   (C)   (D)

(17)

(A)   (B)   (C)   (D)

Correct Answers

(You'll learn more by writing your own answers before comparing them with these.)

1. A	5. C	9. C	13. C
2. C	6. A	10. A	14. C
3. C	7. D	11. D	15. B
4. B	8. B	12. B	16. A
			17. A

Practice Using Answer Sheets

Alter numbers to match the practice and drill questions in each part of the book.
Make only ONE mark for each answer. Additional and stray marks may be counted as mistakes.
In making corrections, erase errors COMPLETELY. Make glossy black marks.

HIDDEN FIGURES

This spatial relations test, sometimes called an "embedded figures test," presents a simple geometric pattern and requires the candidate to find it in a larger, more complete pattern which is sometimes a three-dimensional figure.

In some versions of the test the background is colored irregularly to increase confusion. We have not attempted here to increase your confusion.

In this Practice Chapter you are provided with a set of five simple figures labelled A, B, C, D and E. Then you will find a number of more complex figures which are numbered beginning with one. Next to each figure you are to write the letter of the simple figure which is found hidden or embedded in the more complex figure.................................Each test consists of facing pages, so that in answering questions the simple figures are constantly before you.

HIDDEN FIGURES TEST I

Simple Figures

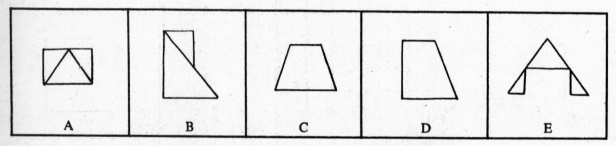

Find The Simple Figures Hidden In These More Complex Figures.

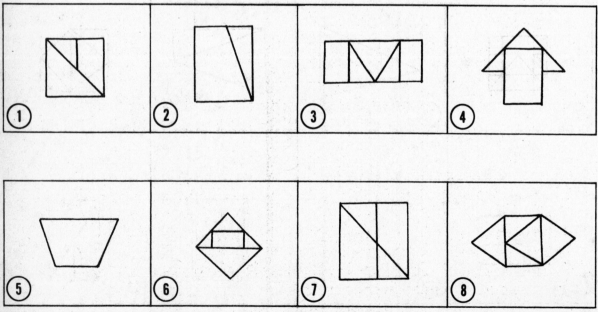

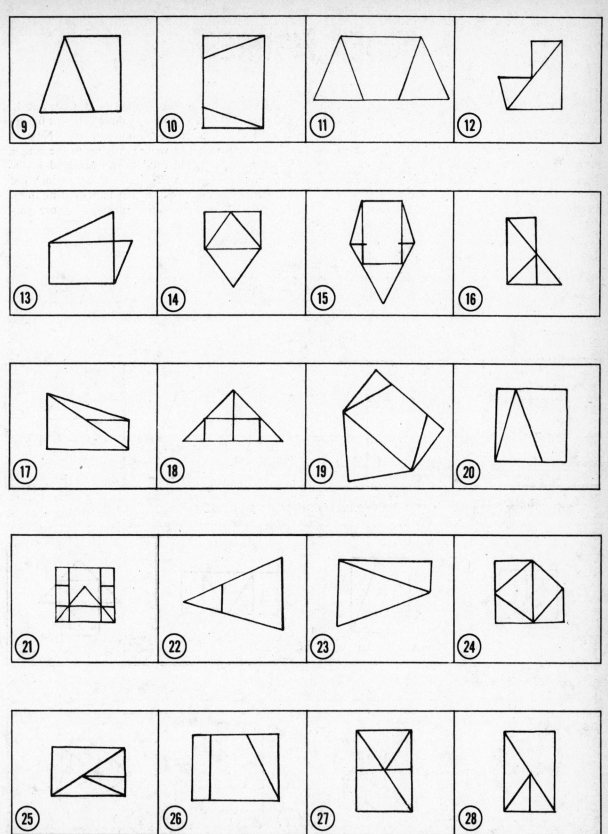

HIDDEN FIGURES TEST II

Simple Figures

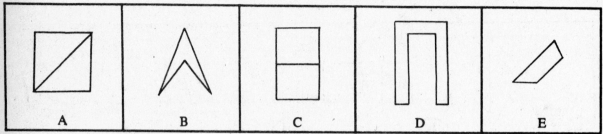

A   B   C   D   E

Find The Simple Figures Hidden In These More Complex Figures.

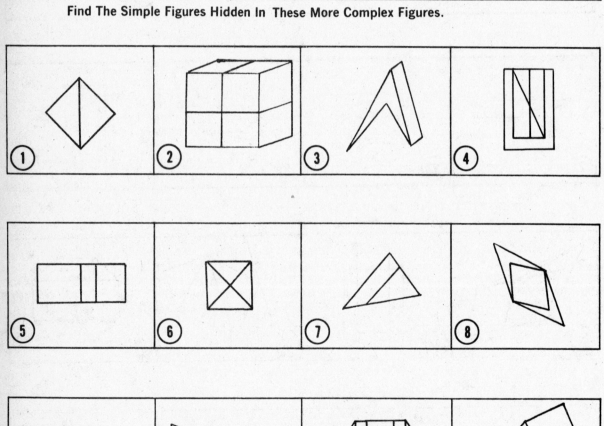

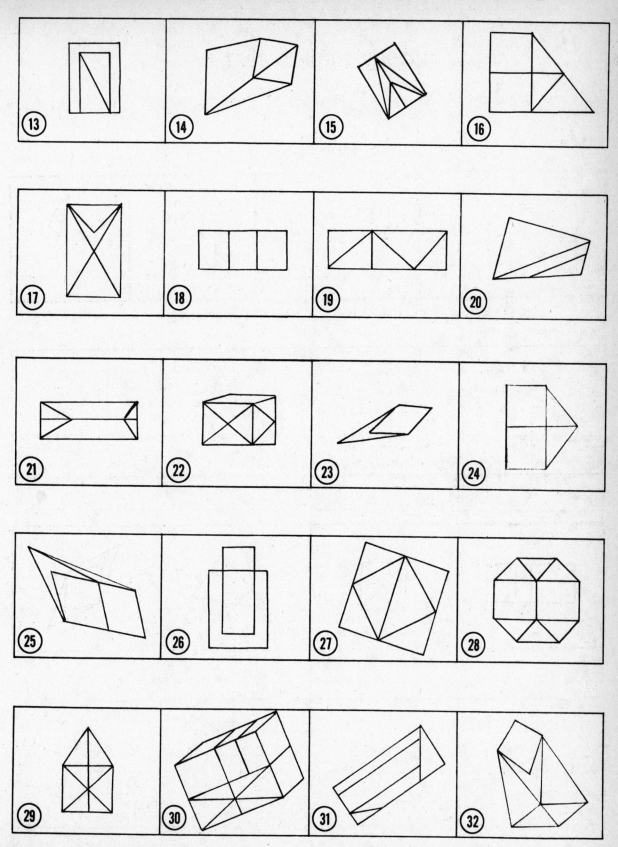

Correct Answers For The Foregoing Questions

(Please try to answer the questions on your own before looking at our answers. You'll do much better on your test if you follow this rule.)

TEST I

1. B	15. E
2. D	16. B
3. A	17. B
4. E	18. E
5. C	19. C
6. E	20. D
7. B	21. E
8. A	22. C
9. D	23. D
10. C	24. A
11. C	25. B
12. B	26. D
13. D	27. A
14. A	28. B

TEST II

1. A	15. B	29. A
2. C	16. C	30. C
3. B	17. B	31. E
4. D	18. C	32. B
5. C	19. A	
6. A	20. E	
7. E	21. E	
8. B	22. A	
9. B	23. B	
10. A	24. C	
11. D	25. B	
12. C	26. D	
13. D	27. A	
14. A	28. C	

SCORE 1 .... %
NO. CORRECT ÷
NO. OF QUESTIONS ON THIS TEST

SCORE 2 .... %
NO. CORRECT ÷
NO. OF QUESTIONS ON THIS TEST

TEST – TAKING MADE SIMPLE

Having gotten this far, you're almost an expert test-taker because you have now mastered the subject matter of the test. Proper preparation is the real secret. The pointers on the next few pages will take you the rest of the way by giving you the strategy employed on tests by those who are most successful in this not-so-mysterious art.

BEFORE THE TEST

T-DAY MINUS SEVEN

You're going to pass this examination because you have received the best possible preparation for it. But, unlike many others, you're going to give the best possible account of yourself by acquiring the rare skill of effectively using your knowledge to answer the examination questions.

First off, get rid of any negative attitudes toward the test. You have a negative attitude when you view the test as a device to "trip you up" rather than an opportunity to show how effectively you have learned.

APPROACH THE TEST WITH SELF-CONFIDENCE. Plugging through this book was no mean job, and now that you've done it you're probably better prepared than 90% of the others. Self-confidence is one of the biggest strategic assets you can bring to the testing room.

Nobody likes tests, but some poor souls permit themselves to get upset or angry when they see what they think is an unfair test. The expert doesn't. He keeps calm and moves right ahead, knowing that everyone is taking the same test. Anger, resentment, fear . . . they all slow you down. "Grin and bear it!"

Besides, every test you take, including this one, is a valuable experience which improves your skill. Since you will undoubtedly be taking other tests in the years to come, it may help you to regard this one as training to perfect your skill.

Keep calm; there's no point in panic. If you've done your work there's no need for it; and if you haven't, a cool head is your very first requirement.

Why be the frightened kind of student who enters the examination chamber in a mental coma? A test taken under mental stress does not provide a fair measure of your ability. At the very least, this book has removed for you some of the fear and mystery that surrounds examinations. A certain amount of concern is normal and good, but excessive worry saps your strength and keenness. In other words, be prepared EMOTIONALLY.

Pre-Test Review

If you know any others who are taking this test, you'll probably find it helpful to review the book and your notes with them. The group should be small, certainly not more than four. Team study at this stage should seek to review the material in a different way than you learned it originally; should strive for an exchange of ideas between you and the other members of the group; should be selective in sticking to important ideas; should stress the vague and the unfamiliar rather than that which you all know well; should be businesslike and devoid of any nonsense; should end as soon as you get tired.

One of the *worst* strategies in test taking is to do *all* your preparation the night before the exam. As a reader of this book, you have scheduled and spaced your study properly so as not to suffer from the fatigue and emotional disturbance that comes from cramming the night before.

Cramming is a very good way to *guarantee poor test results*.

However, you would be wise to prepare yourself factually by *reviewing your notes* in the 48 hours preceding the exam. You shouldn't have to spend more than two or three hours in this way. Stick to salient points. The others will fall into place quickly.

Don't confuse cramming with a final, calm review which helps you focus on the significant areas of this book and further strengthens your confidence in your ability to handle the test questions. In other words, prepare yourself FACTUALLY.

Keep Fit

Mind and body work together. Poor physical condition will lower your mental efficiency. In preparing for an examination, observe the common-sense rules of health. Get sufficient sleep and rest, eat proper foods, plan recreation and exercise. In relation to health and examinations, two cautions are in order. Don't miss your meals prior to an examination in order to get extra time for study. Likewise, don't miss your regular sleep by sitting up late to "cram" for the examination. Cramming is an attempt to learn in a very short period of time what should have been learned through regular and consistent study. Not only are these two habits detrimental to health, but seldom do they pay off in terms of effective learning. It is likely that you will be *more confused* than better prepared on the day of the examination if you have broken into your daily routine by missing your meals or sleep.

On the night before the examination go to bed at your regular time and try to get a good night's sleep. Don't go to the movies. Don't date. In other words, prepare yourself PHYSICALLY.

T-HOUR MINUS ONE

After a very light, leisurely meal, get to the examination room ahead of time, perhaps ten minutes early . . . but not so early that you have time to get into an argument with others about what's going to be asked on the exam, etc. The reason for coming early is to help you get accustomed to the room. It will help you to a better start.

Bring all necessary equipment . . .

. . . pen, two sharpened pencils, watch, paper, eraser, ruler, and any other things you're instructed to bring.

Get settled . . .

. . . by finding your seat and staying in it. If no special seats have been assigned, take one in the front to facilitate the seating of others coming in after you.

The test will be given by a test supervisor who reads the directions and otherwise tells you what to do. The people who walk about passing out the test papers and assisting with the examination are test proctors. If you're not able to see or hear properly notify the supervisor or a proctor. If you have any other difficulties during the examination, like a defective test booklet, scoring pencil, answer sheet; or if it's too hot or cold or dark or drafty, let them know. You're entitled to favorable test conditions, and if you don't have them you won't be able to do your best. Don't be a crank, but don't be shy either. An important function of the proctor is to see to it that you have favorable test conditions.

Relax . . .

. . . and don't bring on unnecessary tenseness by worrying about the difficulty of the examination. If necessary wait a minute before beginning to write. If you're still tense, take a couple of deep breaths, look over your test equipment, or do something which will take your mind away from the examination for a moment.

If your collar or shoes are tight, loosen them.

Put away unnecessary materials so that you have a good, clear space on your desk to write freely.

You Must Have
TO GIVE YOUR Best Test PERFORMANCE

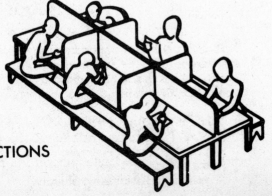

(1) A GOOD TEST ENVIRONMENT

(2) A COMPLETE UNDERSTANDING OF DIRECTIONS

(3) A DESIRE TO DO YOUR BEST

WHEN THEY SAY "GO" — TAKE YOUR TIME!

Listen very carefully to the test supervisor. If you fail to hear something important that he says, you may not be able to read it in the written directions and may suffer accordingly.

If you don't understand the directions you have heard or read, raise your hand and inform the proctor. Read carefully the directions for *each* part of the test before beginning to work on that part. If you skip over such directions too hastily, you may miss a main idea and thus lose credit for an entire section.

Get an Overview of the Examination

After reading the directions carefully, look over the entire examination to get an over-view of the nature and scope of the test. The purpose of this over-view is to give you some idea of the nature, scope, and difficulty of the examination.

It has another advantage. An item might be so phrased that it sets in motion a chain of thought that might be helpful in answering other items on the examination.

Still another benefit to be derived from reading all the items before you answer any is that the few minutes involved in reading the items gives you an opportunity to relax before beginning the examination. This will make for better concentration. As you read over these items the first time, check those whose answers immediately come to you. These will be the ones you will answer first. Read each item carefully before answering. It is a good practice to read each item at least twice to be sure that you understand it.

Plan Ahead

In other words, you should know precisely where you are going before you start. You should know:
1. whether you have to answer all the questions or whether you can choose those that are easiest for you;
2. whether all the questions are easy; (there may be a pattern of difficult, easy, etc.)
3. The length of the test; the number of questions;
4. The kind of scoring method used;
5. Which questions, if any, carry extra weight;
6. What types of questions are on the test;
7. What directions apply to each part of the test;
8. Whether you must answer the questions consecutively.

Budget Your Time Strategically!

Quickly figure out how much of the allotted time you can give to each section and still finish ahead of time. Don't forget to figure on the time you're investing in the overview. Then alter your schedule so that you can spend more time on those parts that count most. Then, if you can, plan to spend less time on the easier questions, so that you can devote the time saved to the harder questions. Figuring roughly, you should finish half the questions when half the allotted time has gone by. If there are 100 questions and you have three hours, you should have finished 50 questions after one and one half hours. So bring along a watch whether the instructions call for one or not. Jot down your "exam budget" and stick to it INTELLIGENTLY.

EXAMINATION STRATEGY

Probably the most important single strategy you can learn is to do the easy questions first. The very hard questions should be read and temporarily postponed. Identify them with a dot and return to them later.

This strategy has several advantages for you:
1. You're sure to get credit for all the questions you're sure of. If time runs out, you'll have all the sure shots, losing out only on those which you might have missed anyway.

2. By reading and laying away the tough ones you give your subconscious a chance to work on them. You may be pleasantly surprised to find the answers to the puzzlers popping up for you as you deal with related questions.

3. You won't risk getting caught by the time limit just as you reach a question you know really well.

THE GIST OF TEST STRATEGY

- APPROACH THE TEST CONFIDENTLY. TAKE IT CALMLY.

- REMEMBER TO REVIEW, THE WEEK BEFORE THE TEST.

- DON'T "CRAM." BE CAREFUL OF YOUR DIET AND SLEEP
  .. ESPECIALLY AS THE TEST DRAWS NIGH.

- ARRIVE ON TIME ... AND READY.

- CHOOSE A GOOD SEAT. GET COMFORTABLE AND RELAX.

- BRING THE COMPLETE KIT OF "TOOLS" YOU'LL NEED.

- LISTEN CAREFULLY TO ALL DIRECTIONS.

- APPORTION YOUR TIME INTELLIGENTLY WITH AN "EXAM BUDGET."

- READ ALL DIRECTIONS CAREFULLY. TWICE IF NECESSARY.
  PAY PARTICULAR ATTENTION TO THE SCORING PLAN.

- LOOK OVER THE WHOLE TEST BEFORE ANSWERING ANY QUESTIONS.

- START RIGHT IN, IF POSSIBLE. STAY WITH IT. USE
  EVERY SECOND EFFECTIVELY.

- DO THE EASY QUESTIONS FIRST; POSTPONE HARDER QUESTIONS
  UNTIL LATER.

- DETERMINE THE PATTERN OF THE TEST QUESTIONS.
  IF IT'S HARD-EASY ETC., ANSWER ACCORDINGLY.

- READ EACH QUESTION CAREFULLY. MAKE SURE YOU UNDERSTAND
  EACH ONE BEFORE YOU ANSWER. RE-READ, IF NECESSARY.

- THINK! AVOID HURRIED ANSWERS. GUESS INTELLIGENTLY.

- WATCH YOUR WATCH AND "EXAM BUDGET," BUT DO A
  LITTLE BALANCING OF THE TIME YOU DEVOTE TO EACH QUESTION.

- GET ALL THE HELP YOU CAN FROM "CUE" WORDS.

- REPHRASE DIFFICULT QUESTIONS FOR YOURSELF.
  WATCH OUT FOR "SPOILERS."

- REFRESH YOURSELF WITH A FEW, WELL-CHOSEN REST
  PAUSES DURING THE TEST.

- USE CONTROLLED ASSOCIATION TO SEE THE RELATION OF
  ONE QUESTION TO ANOTHER AND WITH AS MANY IMPORTANT
  IDEAS AS YOU CAN DEVELOP.

- NOW THAT YOU'RE A "COOL" TEST-TAKER, STAY CALM
  AND CONFIDENT THROUGHOUT THE TEST. DON'T LET
  ANYTHING THROW YOU.

- EDIT, CHECK, PROOFREAD YOUR ANSWERS. BE A "BITTER
  ENDER." STAY WORKING UNTIL THEY
  MAKE YOU GO.

HOW TO BE A MASTER TEST TAKER

FOR FURTHER STUDY

ARCO BOOKS FOR MORE HELP

Now what? You've read and studied the whole book, and there's still time before you take the test. You're probably better prepared than most of your competitors, but you may feel insecure about one or more of the probable test subjects.

Perhaps you've discovered that you are weak in language, verbal ability or mathematics. Why flounder and fail when help is so easily available? Why not brush up in the privacy of your own home with one of these books?

And why not consider the other opportunities open to you? Look over the list and make plans for your future. Start studying for other tests *now*. You can then pick and choose your *ideal* position, instead of settling for the first *ordinary* job that comes along.

Each of the following books was created under the same expert editorial supervision that produced the excellent book you are now using. Though we only list titles and prices, you can be sure that each book performs a real service, and keeps you from fumbling and from failure. Whatever your goal. . . Civil Service, Trade License, Teaching, Professional License, Scholarships, Entrance to the School of your choice. . .you can achieve it through the proven Question and Answer Method.

S3709

CIVIL SERVICE AND TEST PREPARATION—GENERAL

MILITARY EXAMINATION SERIES

HIGH SCHOOL AND COLLEGE PREPARATION

PROFESSIONAL CAREER EXAM SERIES

Action Guide for Executive Job Seekers and Employers, Uris .... _____ 01787-2 3.95
Air Traffic Controller, Morrison .... _____ 04593-0 8.00
Automobile Mechanic Certification Tests, Sharp .... _____ 03809-8 6.00
Bar Exams .... _____ 01124-6 5.00
The C.P.A. Exam: Accounting by the "Parallel Point"
   Method, Lipscomb .... _____ 02020-2 15.00
Certified General Automobile Mechanic, Turner .... _____ 02900-5 6.00
Computer Programmer, Luftig .... _____ 01232-3 8.00
Computers and Automation, Brown .... _____ 01745-7 5.95
Computers and Data Processing Examinations:
   CDP/CCP/CLEP .... _____ 04670-8 10.00
Dental Admission Test, Arco Editorial Board .... _____ 04293-1 6.00
Graduate Management Admission Test .... _____ 04360-1 6.00
Graduate Record Examination Aptitude Test .... _____ 00824-5 5.00
Health Insurance Agent (Hospital, Accident, Health, Life) .... _____ 02153-5 5.00
How a Computer System Works, Brown & Workman .... _____ 03424-6 5.95
How to Become a Successful Model—Second Edition, Krem ..... _____ 04508-6 2.95
How to Get Into Medical and Dental School, revised edition,
   Shugar, Shugar & Bauman .... _____ 04095-5 4.00
How to Make Money in Music, Harris & Farrar .... _____ 04089-0 5.95
How to Remember Anything, Markoff, Dubin & Carcel .... _____ 03929-9 5.00
The Installation and Servicing of Domestic
   Oil Burners, Mitchell & Mitchell .... _____ 00437-1 10.00
Instrument Pilot Examination, Morrison .... _____ 04592-2 9.95
Insurance Agent and Broker .... _____ 02149-7 8.00
Law School Admission Test, Candrilli & Slawsky .... _____ 03946-9 6.00
Life Insurance Agent, Snouffer .... _____ 04306-7 8.00
Medical College Admission Test, Turner .... _____ 04289-3 6.00
Miller Analogies Test—1400 Analogy Questions .... _____ 01114-9 5.00
National Career Directory .... _____ 04510-8 5.95
The 1978-79 Airline Guide to Stewardess and
   Steward Careers, Morton .... _____ 04350-4 5.95
Notary Public .... _____ 00180-1 6.00
Nursing School Entrance Examinations, Turner .... _____ 01202-1 6.00
Oil Burner Installer .... _____ 00096-1 8.00
The Official 1978-79 Guide to Airline Careers, Morton .... _____ 03955-8 5.95
Playground and Recreation Director's Handbook .... _____ 01096-7 8.00
Principles of Data Processing, Morrison .... _____ 04268-0 7.50
Psychology: A Graduate Review, Ozehosky & Polz .... _____ 04136-6 10.00
Real Estate License Examination, Gladstone .... _____ 03755-5 6.00
Real Estate Mathematics Simplified, Shulman .... _____ 04713-5 5.00
Refrigeration License Manual, Harfenist .... _____ 02726-6 10.00
Resumes for Job Hunters, Shykind .... _____ 03961-2 5.00
Resumes That Get Jobs, revised edition, Resume Service .... _____ 03909-4 3.00
Simplify Legal Writing, Biskind .... _____ 03801-2 5.00
Spanish for Nurses and Allied Health Science Students,
   Hernandez-Miyares & Alba .... _____ 04127-7 10.00
Stationary Engineer and Fireman .... _____ 00070-8 8.00
Structural Design .... _____ 04549-3 10.00
The Test of English as a Foreign
   Language (TOEFL), Moreno, Babin & Cordes .... _____ 04450-0 8.00
TOEFL Listening Comprehension Cassette .... _____ 04667-8 7.95
Veterinary College Admissions .... _____ 04147-1 10.00
Your Resume—Key to a Better Job, Corwen .... _____ 03733-4 4.00

ADVANCED GRE SERIES

Biology: Advanced Test for the G.R.E., Solomon .... _____ 04310-5 4.95
Business: Advanced Test for the G.R.E., Berman,
   Malea & Yearwood .... _____ 01599-3 4.95
Chemistry: Advanced Test for the G.R.E., Weiss .... _____ 01069-X 4.95
Economics: Advanced Test for the G.R.E., Zabrenski &
   Heydari-Darafshian .... _____ 04548-5 5.95

Education: Advanced Test for the G.R.E., ... _____ 04117-3 6.
Engineering: Advanced Test for the G.R.E., Ingham & Nesbitt .... _____ 01604-3 4.
French: Advanced Test for the G.R.E., Dethierry .... _____ 01070-3 5.
Geography: Advanced Test for the G.R.E., White .... _____ 01710-4 3.
Geology: Advanced Test for the G.R.E., Dolgoff .... _____ 01071-1 3.
History: Advanced Test for the G.R.E., ... _____ 04414-4 5.
Literature: Advanced Test for the G.R.E. .... _____ 01073-8 3.
Mathematics: Advanced Test for the G.R.E., Bramson .... _____ 04264-8 4.
Music: Advanced Test for the G.R.E., Murphy .... _____ 01471-7 3
Philosophy: Advanced Test for the G.R.E., Steiner .... _____ 01472-5 4.
Physical Education: Advanced Test for the G.R.E., Rubinger .... _____ 01609-4 3.
Physics: Advanced Test for the G.R.E., Bruenn .... _____ 01074-6 3
Political Science: Advanced Test for the G.R.E.,
   Meador & Stewart .... _____ 01459-8 3
Psychology: Advanced Test for the G.R.E., Millman & Nisbett .... _____ 01145-9 4
Sociology: Advanced Test for the G.R.E.,
   .... _____ 04547-7 5
Spanish: Advanced Test for the G.R.E., Jassey .... _____ 01075-4 3
Speech: Advanced Test for the G.R.E., Graham .... _____ 01526-8 3

GRADUATE FOREIGN LANGUAGE TESTS

Graduate School Foreign Language Test: French,
   Kretschmer .... _____ 01461-X 4
Graduate School Foreign Language Test: German, Goldberg ..... _____ 01460-1 3
Graduate School Foreign Language Test: Spanish,
   Hampares & Jassey .... _____ 01874-7 3

PROFESSIONAL ENGINEER EXAMINATIONS

Chemical Engineering, Coren...................................... _____ 01256-0 8
Civil Engineering Technician .... _____ 04267-2 10
Electrical Engineering Technician .... _____ 04149-8 10
Engineer in Training Examination (EIT), Morrison .... _____ 04009-2 10
Engineering Fundamentals .... _____ 04273-7 10
Fundamentals of Engineering, Home Study Program, (3 Vols.) .. _____ 04302-4 45
Fundamentals of Engineering (Vol. I), Morrison .... _____ 04234-6 17
Fundamentals of Engineering (Vol. II), Morrison .... _____ 04240-0 17
Fundamentals of Engineering (2 vols.)............................ _____ 04243-5 35
Industrial Engineering Technician .... _____ 04154-4 10
Mechanical Engineering Technician .... _____ 04274-5 10
Principles and Practice of Electrical
   Engineering Examination, Morrison .... _____ 04031-9 10
Professional Engineer (Civil) State Board
   Examination Review, Packer et al .... _____ 03637-0 15
Professional Engineering Registration: Problems
   and Solutions .... _____ 04269-9 10
Solid Mechanics, Morrison .... _____ 04409-8 10

NATIONAL TEACHER AREA EXAMS

Early Childhood Education: Teaching Area Exam
   for the National Teacher Examination .... _____ 01637-X
Education in the Elementary School: Teaching Area
   Exam for the National Teacher Examination .... _____ 01318-4
English Language and Literature: Teaching Area
   Exam for the National Teacher Examination .... _____ 01319-2
Mathematics: Teaching Area Exam for the
   National Teacher Examination .... _____ 01639-6
National Teacher Examination .... _____ 00823-7